Who's behind the
MASK?

Who's behind the MASK?

Become Who You Have Always Been but Were Never Allowed to Be

A ALLEN M MCCRAY

WHO'S BEHIND THE MASK?
BECOME WHO YOU HAVE ALWAYS BEEN
BUT WERE NEVER ALLOWED TO BE

iUniverse books may be ordered through booksellers or by contacting:

iUniverse LLC
1663 Liberty Drive
Bloomington, IN 47403
www.iuniverse.com
1-800-Authors (1-800-288-4677)

ISBN: 978-1-4917-3877-1 (sc)
ISBN: 978-1-4917-3878-8 (e)

Library of Congress Control Number: 2014911679

Printed in the United States of America.

iUniverse rev. date: 09/04/2014

Contents

Introduction

While I believe anyone can benefit from the material presented in *Who's behind the Mask?,* most of my work has been with people of faith who have struggled with their identities as believers and not gained all they had hoped for from their experiences.

Unfortunately, many faith-based disciplines and churches call us to a standardization or conformity of faith rather than an authentic transformational experience. I have written this book to help readers become who they were created to be.

It is the product of my life experience, training, and hours of working with people on many different levels. I am passionate about this information because of its profound impact on my own life.

I spent many years in the grip of anger. When my wife and I were dating, she would ask me, "Why are you angry?" I would give the typical defensive response *"I am not angry."* As time went on, the anger spilled over into more areas of my life. I often internalized the anger, which, for my personality type, looks like depression. So I was angry and depressed.

I worked hard to compensate for my anger by doing more of everything—work, school, performance, more work, more school, more performance, etc.

My calling and vocation as a pastor was negatively affected by my anger. Needing to be seen as successful and perfect fueled my anger and depression like gasoline on a fire. I vividly remember the day I said to my wife that something had to change: "I can't keep living like this. I don't want to be angry, I don't like who I am, but I don't know what to do."

I could not seem to enjoy life on any level. It was suggested that I get a hobby, have some fun, and play a little. Play was not even in my vocabulary. I tried to take up the game of golf. I would go to the golf course and feel so guilty that I would leave the course and go home and work. I wanted to enjoy life but couldn't get past the guilt and self-condemnation.

I had the opportunity to enroll in a graduate school for counseling. I hoped this would supply me with the answers I was looking for. It was an amazing experience and has had a positive impact on my life, even to this day. However, while I learned to manage my anger and depression, it did not give me the transformation that I was looking for. I had earned two graduate degrees in counseling but still needed answers.

I had received a brochure in the mail to attend a Personality Plus training seminar by Florence Littauer. It was one of those invitations that wouldn't go away. I just kept hanging on to it, until one day, Sharon, my wife, asked me, "What are you going to do with this advertisement?" I said, "Just throw it away; I don't need it." She said, "You have kept it for some reason—maybe you should check it out."

I completed the requirements to attend the training, which required a personality profile that identified me as having a choleric, melancholy personality behavioral style, or, in the language of the DISC, a D/C style. Time and introspection would soon reveal that I was masking the C personality style and denying my natural I personality style, which resulted in an interpersonal conflict that was producing the anger that was controlling my life.

Florence challenged me to reevaluate my responses to the profile. I assured her that I had taken many such assessments and they all revealed the same results. This is where it gets interesting. She challenged me to go home and look at my childhood pictures. In doing so, I found that prior to age seven, I was this happy, fun-loving child with a contagious smile (see figure 1). After the age of seven, my pictures changed dramatically, and so did my personality. I was sad, serious, fearful, and void of life (see figure 2). As I got older, you could see the anger in my face and body language.

figure 1   figure 2

There was a dramatic, life-changing event at the age of seven. My mother passed away at the age of twenty-seven. She was born with a heart defect and was warned not to have children. She had two sons, and although she died at an early age, she outlived the prognosis.

As I began to unpack this childhood trauma, I realized I had internalized Mom's death as being my fault. Mom's last days were spent in our small, five-room house—two bedrooms, a living room, and a bathroom tucked in between one of the bedrooms and the kitchen. Mom's last day was marked by family members arriving, along with the family doctor, who had informed the adults that Mom would not last much longer and that there was nothing else he could do. The stress for the adults was high, and my cousins and I were put in the bedroom next to Mom's to spare us from the tension of the impending death. As children will do, we got loud as we played together, unaware of the seriousness of the situation. My aunt would come to the door and tell us to be quiet so Mom could rest. Again our noise level would increase, and the stress level was equally increasing among the adults. My aunt's next trip to our room was characterized by a higher level of stress, and with a stern voice she said, "Allen, if you don't stop making so much noise and having fun, your mother is going to die." Obviously, she did not understand the magnitude of what she had said, as she and all the other adults were feeling the impending death of their loved one. The next time my aunt came to the room, she took me outside and said, "Allen, I hate to tell you this, but your mother has died."

Little did I know that from that day forward I would feel responsible for my mother's death. I took on a different personality style; having fun (the primary need of my personality style) was not to be in my life.

Perfection would become the order of my life. The longer I covered up my true self, the angrier and more depressed I became. It affected every area of my life, as a husband, father, pastor, and person.

As I learned the personality styles and started to embrace my true self, life begin to change. My true identity began to emerge. I must say that it was scary at first. Taking off the mask and embracing my true identity has truly allowed me to become who I had always been but never allowed myself to be.

I trust that as you read this material, it will have the profound effect on you that it has had on me and the thousands of people who I have had the opportunity to share and work with over many years.

Section 1

Chapter 1

Your Internal World

This book is about your favorite subjects: you and the people you love.

Discovering who you really are is a part of the journey of life that ends only when you take your final breath. Whether you know it or not, you are always growing either up or down; there is no standing still. This book can help you grow beyond your current self to become the person you really are and were never allowed to be.

Our world—home, family, school, church, clubs, work, etc.—continually shapes our beliefs and values. When we were children, the values and beliefs of our parents, caregivers, teachers, mentors, family members, and other significant people became incorporated into our belief systems. These internalized values and beliefs, along with our innate personality behavioral styles, shape the way we view and respond to our external and internal worlds.

> Our external world is everything outside us, and our internal world is what we believe about ourselves and how we see and talk to ourselves.

Until we awaken to our personality behavioral styles, we live on autopilot. Without an awareness of *why* we do what we do, we are powerless to make significant changes in our personal, professional, and relational lives. Consequently, each of us is on a journey that spans both our internal and external worlds.

> Your life's journey is more than mere existence—it is intended to lead you to your destiny!

Life Impact Seminars and this book are dedicated to helping you discover the *real you* by providing understanding about the values and beliefs that reinforce both your positive and negative behaviors. As we learn which values, beliefs, and behaviors are sabotaging our future, we can unlock the potential that is within. Most people believe they are capable of a better quality of life, and they don't know why their past efforts to improve themselves have failed. However, that can change, and the change can start today.

After more than thirty years of teaching this material, I have seen thousands of lives changed, broken marriages healed, estranged families reunited, and new careers launched. This is not a pill that magically creates change; however, miracles will happen as you learn to be self-aware.

Learning to hear the "still small voice" (1 Kings 19:12) resonating within your soul will bring greater depth, value, meaning, and fulfillment to this journey called life. Now is your time to stop living on autopilot and pursue your purpose for being here.

> Fasten your seatbelt and get ready for an incredible journey to find your purpose and destiny.

The Window of the Soul

This window can help us know and understand the *needs of the soul*. When those needs are not met, we are impoverished. When they are met, we prosper. "I pray that you may prosper in *all things* and be in health, just as *your soul prospers*" (3 John 1:2 NKJV; italics added). This verse is crucial to understanding that the soul's health determines how we handle *all things*, including every aspect of life: physical health, wealth, poverty, relationships, discouragements, victories, losses, family, etc.

Living life to our full potential does not necessarily come from experiences or by gathering information. Something more is required.

> Being informed is not the same as being transformed.

Transformation becomes possible only when we develop the ability to understand our moods, emotions, and drives as well as their effects on others. These are the beginning steps on the pathway to genuine transformation. The next step is to understand the hunger pains of the soul.

> The soul hungers for what cannot be bought and thirsts for what the world cannot provide.

Too often, we try to feed the soul by satisfying the needs of the ego, such as the need to be seen as successful based on our jobs, titles, social status, or wealth. While evaluating these things is not wrong, pursuing them will not satisfy the hunger pains of the soul, such as the need for belonging, love, intimacy, and identity, to mention a few.

When the soul's needs are not met, we develop unhealthy behaviors to try to satisfy those needs. The more impoverished the soul, the more destructive and pathological the behavior becomes. (We will discuss this more in later chapters.)

> When we try to meet the soul's needs by satisfying the appetites of the ego, we are feeding junk food to the soul.

What Is the Soul?

The soul may be the most difficult part of a person to describe. It is the core of our being. It separates us from every other living creature; I am speaking of the eternal part of ourselves. The soul is our divine part. It is God's breath within us. According to the Creation story, God formed man from the dust of the ground and breathed into his nostrils the breath of life, and man became a living soul (Genesis 2:7).

> The soul is not a thing but a quality or a dimension of experiencing life and ourselves. It has to do with the depth of living, value, relatedness, heart, and personal substance.[1]

To attain and maintain physical, emotional, and mental health, we must find completeness and wholeness of the spirit, soul, and body and then nurture them to keep them fit. To tend to our bodies with exercise and our spirits with religion but leave out the wellness of the soul is like trying to balance life on a two-legged stool. This book is all about tending the needs of the soul.

Understanding Ourselves: An Overview

For this study, we will use a personality behavioral model to assist us in our voyage of self-discovery. This personality model is simply a window into the soul; it is not the totality of whom we are any more than a window shows the entirety of a house. However, it is a way of seeing ourselves in relation to others and understanding how we communicate and receive information. When we look out this window of personality behavioral styles, we see how we view the world. When we look in this window, we see how the world views us.

The modern understanding of personality behavior styles is based on the work of Hippocrates, circa 400 BC. The father of medicine observed the behaviors of his patients and categorized the way they viewed the world and how the world viewed them. He identified four basic personality behavior styles and named them with words familiar to a physician:

- choleric
- sanguine
- phlegmatic
- melancholy

Modern applications use various other designations, including the DISC-language terms:

- D for decisive (choleric)
- I for influential (sanguine)

- S for steady (phlegmatic)
- C for cautious (melancholy)

Some writers and speakers use colors, animals, or other metaphors to convey the personality types, but this book will use the more modern DISC language for clarity. I also will use *personality styles* and *behavior styles* interchangeably to describe these behavioral patterns. The following list reflects the basic behaviors of the four personality styles.

1. We will look at those who score in the high range of the *decisive* (D) profile. These people tend to be direct, and they move quickly to solve new problems. They like the challenge of a task to be conquered. These highly energetic and task-oriented people gain energy from their work. They speak with authority and use straightforward language. The Nike slogan exemplifies high D language: "Just do it!"

    The high D is often a great source of innovation and new solutions to problems. This person loves a good challenge, freedom, and variety.

2. The *influential* (I) personality is popular, fun-loving, and sees the world as a place for enjoyment and pleasure, as expressed in the classic line, "Are we having fun yet?" These people gain energy from being with others. To them, a stranger is someone they haven't met yet. They are very persuasive, seek to persuade people with their charm, and often are indirect in their communications style. They might say, "If you have time, would you do it?"

3. The high-scoring *steady* (S) personality is peaceful, stabilizing, and prefers a slower-paced controlled, deliberative, and predictable environment. The

high S demonstrates a strong sense of loyalty to a team or organization, avoids conflict at all cost, and has the lowest energy level of all the styles. People often label those with this personality style as lazy, which is generally untrue. Due to their avoidance of conflict, they often control through procrastination. When dealing with a high S personality, one should never interpret silence as consent. They might say, "Can I help you do it?" or "You don't have to do it if you don't want to."

4. High *cautious* (C) personalities are careful and lean toward perfectionism. People with this style are highly organized and need their world to be orderly. Their careful attention to detail often limits the number of projects they can take on; they prefer to do one thing at a time. High C personality types are susceptible to depression and may use moodiness to control their world. Their energy level is moderate, but they find interacting with people to be emotionally draining. Cautious personalities gain energy from being alone in an orderly environment. They might say, "If you are going to do it, make sure you do it right."

Basic Needs and Drives of Each Personality Style

The fundamental need of the high D is to be in control. These highly driven personalities can follow a leader in whom they have confidence but may run over a leader they find lacking. They will walk into a room full of people and take charge if there appears to be a leadership vacuum. The D needs and seeks recognition for accomplishments and may measure others according to who has the best job, the best education, or the most powerful toys. The egos of high D personalities drive them to play king of the hill, and they believe the end justifies any means to attain their goals.

The basic need of the high I is to have fun. These energetic personalities love to entertain. They walk into a room and light it up; their presence demands attention. They enjoy telling stories about themselves and may give more information than people want to hear. They become bored with lengthy projects; consequently, they rarely finish one before starting another. Their egos are driven by a need for significance through recognition. Popularity is of the utmost importance to them, and they often embellish stories to keep people engaged. They will evaluate others according to how much fun they can have with them.

High S personalities desire peace. This low-energy behavior style conveys a sense of peace and brings calm and tranquility to most situations. Their reluctance to compete often leaves them on the sidelines of conversations. When offered the opportunity, they can make valuable contributions to the decision-making process. They prefer a steady, slow-paced work environment and can be highly productive. Compared to a high I, the high S is like a tortoise in a race with a hare. High S egos are driven by the need for certainty in their relationships, which causes them to avoid confrontations.

The basic need of high C personality types is perfection and order. They seek to be understood. Their classic statement is, "There is a place for everything, and everything in its place." These personalities need spaces of their own and generally feel drained when they have to spend too much time around other people. Their decision-making process is based on facts supported by research. Because relationships are very important to them, they are slow to trust people and do not appreciate strangers invading their personal space. The high C ego is driven by certainty based on facts; therefore, decision making can fall victim to paralysis by analysis.

It should be obvious by now that most of us are more than one personality type. Research reveals that only 1 percent of the population is dominant in one area. While there are four basic types, there are countless combinations due to various factors. Many of these will be discussed in later chapters.

With this brief introduction to the basic four personality styles, I expect that you have already gained insight into yourself and others. Remember, this is a small and incomplete window into the soul. However, I have had the opportunity to teach this material in many different countries and cultures, and I have witnessed the transformation of lives, the healing of broken marriages, the mending of estranged families, and the launching and advancement of powerful careers.

> Nothing is so powerful as insight into human nature . . . what compulsions drive a man, what instincts dominate his actions . . . If you know these things about a man, you can touch him at the core of his being.[2]

Chapter 2

Let's Talk

> You have no doubt heard that the three most important words in real estate are *location, location, location*. Well, the three most important words in a relationship are *communication, communication, communication*.

In addition to the words we speak, we also communicate in three other ways: body language, pace or rate of speaking, and voice intonation. Each personality style has its own unique way of imparting information.

The Dominant Personality Style

High D and C personalities tend to be very direct in their verbal communication, while I and S personality types are indirect.

The high D body language is generally very forceful and may include a lot of finger pointing during conversations. Really powerful Ds often will use two fingers. They may pound their fists on a table or the palms of their hands. This personality uses direct eye contact and prefers speaking face to face. They are like drill sergeants, shouting out orders without giving options, as in, "Take out the trash!" I and S personality styles will use a more indirect approach, such as, "Will you take out the trash?" or "When you have time, please take out the trash."

D personalities walk heavy; you can even hear them coming down a carpeted hallway, and they actually wear out their shoe heels faster than the other personality types wear out theirs. They usually walk as if they are on a mission—heads forward and looking straight ahead, to avoid the distraction of eye contact with others. These personalities can become so task focused that they ignore those closest to them until their mission is completed.

The verbal communication that works best with the high D personality is to convey each task as a challenge, such as:

- This is a winning situation.
- You can lead the field.
- Let's get results.
- Let's do it now.
- Will you accept the challenge?

Verbiage that does not resonate with the D type includes:

- Follow my directions.
- In my opinion . . .

The high D likes direct communication that gets to the bottom line as quickly as possible.

The Influential Personality Style

High I types use animated gestures while talking; they can speak volumes with their eyes and facial expressions. They often speak rapidly and nonstop. They dress in ways that attract attention and often have a flair for fashion. To engage a high I, talk about how much fun and how exciting an event will be. They enjoy small talk and like to answer questions about themselves before they get down to business. They are fond of statements that describe their *feelings*, and they are primarily interested in things that will make them look good.

Language that does not work well with this personality type includes words that describe everyone as equal. They dislike uniforms, because they cannot express themselves through their clothing. Their need for spontaneity and excitement makes them resist things that require a great deal of study or a lot of detail work.

The Steady Personality Style

The body language of a high S type is the opposite of that of the D and I. In fact, the lack of body language often speaks louder than the animation of the I or the forcefulness of the D. The laid-back, peaceful demeanor of the S can be disarming or, at times, intimidating. The S moves and speaks at a slower pace than other personality styles, which is often an irritant to the D and the I. The unobtrusive behavior of this type can be misinterpreted as a lack of interest, and their silence perceived as consent. The S generally dresses for comfort and often avoids situations requiring constrictive clothing, such as formal attire.

S personalities dislike boisterous and emotional language, and they are best engaged through step-by-step instructions and the assurance that they are not operating alone. The S needs the reassurance of credible and specific promises regarding the outcome as well as sufficient time to think about any decision. Verbiage about innovation and winning, especially at the possible cost of a relationship, does not resonate with the high S.

The Cautious Personality Style

Body language of high Cs tends to be closed without flamboyant gestures. They may appear to be protecting themselves and the information they possess. You often can identify Cs by the crispness and neatness of their clothing. They speak clearly and precisely, and, like Ds, they can be intimidatingly direct in their communication. Occasionally, a C may be an eccentric chatty professor (a high C that talks like an I). They have so much information that it overflows, and they can't stop themselves from sharing.

To engage the high C, present the facts and communicate a lack of risk and the use of proven methods. They like to know that analysis has been performed on the proposed project and that the projected results are credible. If you want to bring a high C to your point of view, avoid words like cutting-edge, educated guess, untested, and experimental.

As we continue discovering the personality types and their styles, you will become ever more aware of your own type. This will be especially true when we examine the composite personalities in the next section, because they describe most of us.

> Understanding ourselves is essential to our emotional health.

Composite Personality Types

Now that we have described the four basic personality behavioral styles, we will examine natural and unnatural combinations of those styles.

Research by several universities has verified that we are born with our personalities and then develop our characters. Personality styles are passed on through genetics and are identifiable early in life. I train parents and caregivers to recognize the signs that indicate a child's behavioral style, so they know how to most effectively meet his or her needs.

Natural Combinations

Each personality style, which is created by a combination of personality types, comes with its own unique strengths and weakness. One type is always more dominant than the other, which means one is primary and the other, secondary. Sometimes the prominent type within the combination varies according to the situation.

1. The powerful D and the popular I styles are natural combinations. One of the challenges they face, however, is the difference between the direct communication style of the D and the indirect style of the I. The I side can soften the D's style. Ds can be so task focused that they may use or run over people for the sake of winning, because they may see everything in life as a win/lose situation. However, the I side of the personality is concerned with people, wants everyone to be happy, and

wants to be liked. So, the I complements the D by tempering the latter's aggressiveness.

When the I is the dominant style in this combination, the opposite occurs. The I side can get so caught up in socializing, that it forgets the task at hand. The D side keeps the social butterfly on task and makes certain that everyone is in the loop. This combination makes a win/win situation more feasible.

2. The popular I and the peaceful S make a natural combination. Again, one will generally be primary and the other secondary. One of the challenges is the extroversion of the I and the introversion of the S. I types gets energy from other people, while the S has the lowest energy of all the personalities. The S side slows the I down. The popular I can be overwhelming at times, even to similar personality types. The peaceful S can take the sometimes annoying edge off the I. However, the I gives S types a way to engage the world around them when the S allows the I to come out to play. If the I side of the personality wears out the S, this person may go into hibernation for a while.

3. Another natural combination is the peaceful S and perfect C. Since both styles are introverted, they often are not socially engaged and remain in the background. Making decisions is one of the biggest challenges for this combination. The C's need for certainty of facts and the S's desire for certainty in their relationships can keep this person stuck in a valley of indecision.

    The S's need for certainty in relationships can soften the C's overly critical and perfectionist side. The

C's levelheaded approach can spare the S from overcommitting and agreeing to a plan solely to keep the peace. This combination can be very powerful in maintaining quality in the workplace and value in relationships.

4. The perfectionist C and the powerful D also work well together; both are direct communicators and good at decision making. The D side makes decisions from the gut or at an intuitive level, and the C makes decisions based on research and facts. When both strengths are applied to the equation, the result is powerful. The challenge is to balance the quick decision making of the D with the slower methodical pace of the C.

The extroverted D side may help the introverted C side become more engaged with people. However, the D and C can be so direct, they both may alienate people. The C side will keep the D from overcommitting and always shooting from the hip. Ds can be so confident that they dismiss reality and focus on their projected outcome. When this works, we call it risk taking. When it fails, we call it bad judgment. The C can bring facts to the table that can guide the D's decision making.

Unnatural Combinations

Two primary unnatural combinations cause conflicts within individuals. They sometimes are referred to as me-me conflicts. They are usually the result of external pressure that forces the subconscious to *mask behavior.*

The first conflicting combination is the I/C profile. The popular I and perfect C form an unnatural combination. The I personality type is spontaneous, while the perfect C is calculating. The I trusts people; the C is skeptical. The I gains energy from being with people; the C is drained by people. I types love to elaborate their stories; Cs just want the facts. When these two personality styles appear in one person over an extended period of time, the emotional conflict can create debilitating stress.

The second conflicting combo is the D/S profile. The powerful D and the peaceful S are at opposite ends of the spectrum. Ds makes instinctual, quick decisions, while S types avoid making decisions, fearing the personal price they might have to pay. The D has the highest energy of all the personality styles, and the S, the lowest. The D likes a good fight; the S hates conflict. Ds get energy from having a number of tasks on their plate, while the S prefers doing one thing at a time. Again, when these conflicting styles are present over an extended period of time, the stress level is very high and often results in physical issues.

A way of picturing conflicting profiles is to imagine a person driving a car with one foot on the brake and the other on the gas pedal. After a while, the car will malfunction.

External Conflicts

External conflicts can have a negative impact on any of the personality types, for example, a high I doing the work of a high C, or a high S doing the work of a high D. People often get pushed into job situations that do not fit their behavioral styles. They become stressed out, the quality of their work diminishes, and their productivity declines. People under this kind of stress usually are unhappy, miss work, and become critical of their workplaces.

Any of the personalities can do the work of an opposite personality style for a brief time; for example, I am a high I/D who finds writing exhausting. I was able to do the high C work of research when I wrote papers required by my graduate programs. However, I had to take frequent recreational breaks to restore my energy level so I could finish them.

When we are aware that we need to function in a conflicting style, we can compensate for it. When we don't know that we are operating in a conflicting personality style, that is called *masking*.

There is no evidence that we are born with conflicting personality styles. The stress created when we are driven by two opposing personality types is not natural and overwhelms our systems. The result of this conflict is an *implosion*, which hurts us, or an *explosion*, which harms others.

> Conflicting personality profiles are the result of life's pressures and traumas.

The Causes of Masking

The following descriptions identify ten factors that lead to masking and are adapted from the teaching and training of Florence Littauer, my mentor and the author of many books on personalities, including *Personality Plus*:[3]

1. Domineering parents: These are parents who try to shape the child in their own images or personality behavioral styles, rather than acknowledging and honoring the child's innate personality style. Most parents who do this do not understand differing personalities. An example would be a high D parent who wants to make a high S child see and respond to the world as a D. Another is the high I parent who gets her high C child to respond to people the way she does, rather than acknowledge that the child has a different personality style.

2. Alcoholic parents: When children are forced into the role of caregiver, protector, or enabler, they are blocked from being who they were born to be. To survive, they must take on a personality style to fit the situation.

3. Strong feelings of rejection: A primary human need is the need for belonging. Children who feel unwanted for any reason—e.g., they are the wrong gender, they were unexpected, their birth created a financial burden, etc.—will feel forced to redeem themselves and to become the personality they think the parent or caregiver wants to see.

4. Any form of emotional or physical abuse: Abuse causes the child to seek a behavior that will stop the mistreatment. This creates confusion as the child tries to please the abuser by pretending to be perfect, happy, quiet, defensive, etc. When nothing works, which is usually the case, the child feels hopeless and worthless.

5. Childhood sexual interference or violation: Because children are not physically, mentally, or emotionally ready for sexual activity, this abuse leads to masking.

The child will search for behavior that will stop the perpetrator. The problem is greatly multiplied when the abuser is a parent or a trusted caregiver.

6. Single-parent home: A single-parent home does not in itself cause masking. The masking is produced when expectations are placed on a child although they are inappropriate for his or her age and inconsistent with his or her personality style. For example, a child may be overtly or covertly encouraged to be the little man or little woman of the house.

7. Birth order: Parents may put unrealistic requirements on their firstborn children to conform to idealistic expectations inconsistent with their personalities. When parents' expectations conflict with the child's personality type, the child may put on an unnatural mask of behavior.

8. Legalism, religious homes, or the church: Overly controlling rules that emphasize appearance, performance, and conformity often cause children (and adults) to assume the controlling entity's personality style so they can gain acceptance and approval.

9. Domineering and controlling spouses: You do not have to be a child to put on a mask of conformity to gain approval. It is common for a person to try to please by taking on his or her spouse's personality type. For example, a high S married to a high C may try to become a C to overcome the latter's controlling nature. This never works out well.

10. Other childhood traumas: Any number of traumas may occur in the lives of children, altering personalities and causing masking, including

divorce, death of a parent, parental absence, loss of a sibling, a parent's or their own extended illnesses, loss of security, a bad relationship between the parents, drugs in the home, frequent moves, bullying at school or at home, etc.

It is never too late to become who you were born to be, but it is never too early.

Chapter 3

Emotional Ups and Downs

> The unmet needs of the soul cause unhealthy behavior; the more impoverished the soul, the more destructive and compulsive that behavior.

As we examine the emotional needs of each personality types, we will gain insight into the needs of their souls.

Emotional Needs of the High D Personality

- Loyalty: If this personality type has been disappointed by someone, he or she might make this classic statement: "After all I've done for you . . ."
- Control: The more out of control the D feels, the more aggressive he or she becomes. This behavior can manifest as a power struggle, with verbal, emotional, and sometimes physical abuse. When turned inward, the D will turn to self-abuse—e.g., punishing exercise or extreme work—that may push the body beyond its limits.
- Recognition: Ds thrive on public recognition, certificates of achievement, and trophies. They are not egotistical; although it may degenerate into narcissism; it is merely the way a D is wired.
- Appreciation: The D's soul hungers for acknowledgment of efforts to meet the needs of others. The healthy D can be very generous,

benevolent, and magnanimous, and a thank-you is all that is needed. However, the unhealthy D may be generous, benevolent, and magnanimous for the purpose of control.

Basic Fears of the D

The emotional health of high Ds will determine how in touch they are with their fears. Unhealthy Ds never admit they are fearful and overcompensate to hide their fear. If they are out of control, their fear may manifest as anger, boisterous declarations about past accomplishments, and exaggerations of their present difficulties.

Their fears typically come from things that make them lose control—family struggles, jobs, financial disasters, poor health, aging, and physical incapacity. This sense of loss leads to high stress levels and depression.

Stress and depression look different in the high D than in other personality types. When stressed, high Ds will work harder and for longer hours, look for physical things to do, and avoid situations they think they cannot win. Depressed D types may become increasingly angry and demanding of themselves and others. They may become obsessed with exercising and overdo it as a form of self-punishment. The more out of control they feel, the more ruthless, dictatorial, and terrorizing they can become.

This person would benefit greatly from professional counseling or a life coach but may find it difficult to seek help from others.

Emotional Needs of the High I Personality

- Attention: When high I types enter a room, they demand attention by announcing their arrival, making a dramatic entrance, or by wearing flamboyant clothing. In some cases, they use all of the above. They refuse to be ignored.
- Affection: The soul of the I craves affection, intimacy, and warmth in relationships. This need causes I types to share personal information to a fault. Consequently, their need to be loved makes them overly trusting, and others often take advantage of them.
- Touch: I types find it hard talk to someone without touching a hand, arm, or shoulder. When this need for physical contact is not met in a healthy way, they will seek unhealthy and sometimes sexual extremes instead. The country song "Looking for Love in All the Wrong Places" captures the extremes to which I types will resort. The unhealthy I can become so depraved, this need becomes insatiable. Trying to satisfy this need for love and affection can be like filling a bottomless bucket.
- Approval: I types long for approval of every effort that they make. This need for validation makes them vulnerable to abuse by other personality types.
- Acceptance: It is vitally important that this need for acceptance is understood by the parents, children, spouses, and coworkers of I types. When they are accepted for whom they are, they will seek to improve themselves. When they are not accepted by the significant people in their lives, they become more fixated on gaining attention and acceptance, which often results in negative behaviors.

Basic Fears of the High I

Being unpopular or ignored is their greatest fear; they crave attention. When they think they have lost credibility or the approval of their circle of friends, they will look for new friends. Consequently, other personalities often view high I types as superficial, shallow, and a bit flaky, which unfortunately feeds their fears of being ignored and unpopular.

High I types fear the aging process more than other types do. Getting older and, in their eyes, unattractive is the worst thing that can happen. Often the high I will go to great expense to turn back the clock. We have all seen high I personalities attempt to reverse the signs of aging with less-than-complementary facelifts and work on other parts of their bodies.

Running out of money is another fear. Each personality type has a unique view of money, but for high I types, money is vital for having fun. When they are running out of money, their panic may overcome rational thinking. An example would be a young high I marrying a wealthy older person for financial security.

The fear that they will not have fun (however they define that), have no hope for their desired future, or will be unloved often will cause I types to have high levels of stress and depression. Stress and depression in the I looks different than it does in the other types. High I types may endeavor to relieve stress by shopping therapy, which only makes their financial conditions worse.

I have worked with people who bankrupted their families by compulsive shopping. Some I types give in to other compulsions, such as gambling, eating, drinking, drugs, etc. Their depression may also be expressed by excessive partying.

Depressed I types will not eat just one piece of pie; they will eat the entire pie. The high I in a stressed or depressed state will become distracted, scattered, self-centered, unstable, insatiable, overwhelmed, and emotionally paralyzed.

I types can benefit greatly from professional counseling or coaching, but they often have difficulty staying with the process. They frequently jump from one counselor, life coach, marriage, church, job, or club to another they think will better meet their needs. The counselor or life coach must be very skilled to keep the high I engaged in the treatment process.

Emotional Needs of the High S Personality

- Peace and quiet: Peacefulness is a quality that radiates from the S personality types. In childhood, they are the pleasant children, easy to care for and often overlooked. You can spot them in a movie script as the peaceful, calm people in the midst of chaos. Sandra Bullock's character in the movie *While You Were Sleeping* is a prime example of the S personality style. You may recognize the high S as the calm TV anchor reporting on a great tragedy. S types make great diplomats, because they bring peacefulness to their environments. They change the atmosphere when they enter a room. When their world is not at peace, they will withdraw and seek out a place of tranquility to replenish their energy levels.

- Sense of worth: Being valued is one of the soul needs of the high S. Of all the personality types, the S is most likely to suffer from low self-esteem. The American high D culture does not always value the reserved, introverted quiet demeanor of the S. Consequently, the S often is overlooked, undervalued, and dismissed as not in the game. S types often find their self-worth in their jobs or areas of expertise. Because their souls hunger for significance and competency, if they are unable to find them, they may check out of society by hibernating in their rooms.

- Lack of stress: High S types may pursue peace by avoiding conflict and seek relationships by overcommitting at their personal expense. While this may seem illogical, this style of behavior often will meet one need by avoiding another need. This becomes a conflict in the lives of high S types, because peace is their greatest need. Their need to avoid conflict and stress can be so deep, they may sacrifice themselves on the altar of service to others to gain the stress-free environment they crave.

- Self-respect: S types often sacrifice their need for self-respect by becoming doormats in order to avoid conflict or an angry person. This contradictory behavior reinforces the lack of self-respect and further aggravates the issue. Merely making S types aware of their need will not help; in fact, it can frighten them. Their souls cannot become nourished until their hunger for a lack of stress is met. When this takes place, high S types can make a positive impact on their world.

Emotional Fears of the High S

The preceding descriptors make S types sound weak and insecure; they are insecure, yes; but weak, no! In fact, the high S is very strong and can be extremely resolute. As we look at the emotional fears of this style, we will gain clues to its power.

Being pressured to work creates continuous fear. The high S is not afraid of work but dreads being overwhelmed by it. Unlike the high D, tasks do not give the high S energy, which comes only from peace and quiet. Consequently, high S types work best when they can focus on one job at a time.

The metaphor "left holding the bag" describes the high S type's fear of being held completely responsible for things that do not go well. Therefore, the S may withhold information to retain the upper hand. The S fears conflicts that appear overwhelming. The stress of confrontation can be so great that it is paralyzing, which can create a domino effect that causes the high S to further lose confidence. This in turn produces a lack of self-respect that results in the S feeling a lack of self-worth.

The fears of the high S produce overwhelming stress levels and often lead to depression. Because high S types are so introverted and have such quiet and peaceful demeanors, it can be hard to detect when they are depressed. A few clues are excessive TV watching, overeating, and checking out of life.

Coworkers brought a high S client to me when they found him sitting at his desk, staring into space, and unresponsive when they called his name. When he arrived at my office, we made him comfortable, and I asked him simple questions. However, he was unable to give definitive answers to questions such as his favorite color, food, or drink. His only answer was, "I don't know." No doubt he had been in a state of depression for some time, but his quiet demeanor hid his condition until he was completely overwhelmed.

The high S can benefit from a life coach or counselor who is skilled at leading the client into self-awareness and gives precise tools for transformation.

Emotional Needs of the High C Personality

- High sensitivity to personal feelings: High C personality types experience their emotions more deeply than other types do. They often are considered overly sensitive, and that may be the case. However, even a healthy C will seem more sensitive and introspective than other personality types. Accordingly, maintaining a healthy level of introspection is not only helpful, it's a necessity for the high C.
- Support when despondent: This soul need is directly tied to the first need, sensitivity. High Cs look for support from the people around them; however, unless a parent, spouse, boss, or friend knows how to give the *right* support, the effort may be counterproductive. For example, a high I will try to support Cs by attempting to cheer them up. The high D will tell them, "Suck it up, pull yourself up by your

boot straps, and tough it out." The C does not need to be cheered up or challenged; this personality type simply needs to be understood. If you are married to a high C or raising one, this one piece of information alone is worth the price of this book. When high Cs feel understood, they will cheer themselves up and even encourage others. When they do not feel understood, they become depressed and moody.

- Space to be alone: High Cs not only need time to be alone, they need their own space in which to be alone. They can be very territorial and possessive of their stuff. If a high C child has to share a room with an high I sibling, there will be problems.

- Silence: The need for space and silence lies deep in the high C's soul, which is how it is nurtured and reenergized. When the soul is not tended to, the high C may be come self-absorbed, temperamental, hateful, self-rejecting, and despairing of life.

- Time alone: As stated above, the high C is drained by people and needs a solitary environment to escape from the crowd. After a gathering at church or a party, the differences between a high C and his or her high I spouse are obvious. The C will go directly to the car, while the social butterfly high I has to make sure everyone gets a hug and a good-bye. I have high C pastor friends who go straight home and hide after a church service until their energy levels are restored.

Basic Fears of the High C Personality

The high C often is haunted by the fear of making a mistake. It is not so much about what other people will think, but more about how the C feels personally. That is why external encouragement is ineffective for this personality type. At a deep level, the fear of making a mistake equates to being a failure. It is a shame-based fear that believes *I made a mistake; therefore, I am a mistake.*

Having to compromise or lower standards is a great obstacle for the high C type. Unfortunately, all of us develop ideal selves that become our subconscious goals. Unless the high C comes to understand that the ideal self is not his or her true identity, any adjustment seems like a compromise. This becomes a vicious circle that continuously sabotages the best efforts of the perfectionist C personality. A skilled counselor or life coach can help end this self-sabotaging behavior.

Another fear high Cs have is that no one will ever understand them. This soul need can only be met internally. Until this need is nurtured within, the high C will have difficulty accepting the understanding and support of others.

The fear that life will not be perfect produces extreme levels of stress in high C personalities. They often argue that a DISC profile that reflects the perfectionist style is incorrect, declaring, "I'm not a high C, because I'm not perfect." The issue, however, is not their perfection, but their need for it.

If you are a C, do not be dismayed. We need high C types in our world; they manage the details of our lives. They write great literature and poetry, produce fine art, and make profound discoveries. The high C population includes most of the world's geniuses, but their personality type also means they bear some of the greatest burdens. They also are the most romantically loyal of all personality types.

Unfortunately, the high C is also the most prone to depression or melancholia, as it is sometimes called. Because their usually somber demeanor can cause the casual observer to miss the deeper signs of depression, watch for excessive alienation, self-indulgence, denying life in general, or excessive hibernation evidenced by reading, studying, or sleeping. This excessiveness causes high Cs to avoid life and gives them the potential to be self-destructive.

Living with Yourself

While this section is focused on descriptions of the four primary personality styles, be assured that we will discuss combinations of these styles in later chapters. We are laying an important foundation for understanding the dynamics of personality combinations as well as the ability to live beyond your personality, which also will be discussed at length.

"Our duty is to be more ourselves, not less."[4]

To paraphrase the early Christian writer Irenaeus, the more fully functioning and vitally alive our personalities are, the more we are able to actualize God's will and our destinies.

Chapter 4

Celebrating Strengths and Understanding Weaknesses

Strengths carried to an extreme become weaknesses

This is an important insight, because often our unconscious, self-sabotaging behaviors keep us stuck in our own personal wildernesses of transition. In this chapter, I will identify the strengths of each of the four styles of behavior and show what happens when those strengths are carried to extremes. The following material is adapted from the teachings of Lance Wallnau in *Train the Trainer* workshops.[5]

The High D Personality's Strengths and Weaknesses

- Goal-oriented: One of the great strengths of high D personality types is that they are goal oriented. The D is very task oriented and good at multitasking. This strength can be carried to an extreme. When Ds are motivated to please or impress others, they may take on too many projects. This can result in impatience and ruthlessness with self and others and produce tunnel vision. By that, I mean they cannot see the needs of people, due to the imperative the project creates within them, or acknowledge any progress that is less than a win or falls short of the success they desire. At a very extreme level, this behavior can degenerate into behaviors that are destructive to themselves or others. High Ds generally seek help only if court ordered or when they are trying to save their marriages or businesses.

- Self-confident: High Ds feel self-reliant, which serves them well until it becomes overly exaggerated. This dominant style believes it can step into any situation and accomplish the goals of the organization, solve problems, and resolve concerns. The good news is they are often successful; the bad news is they are often very successful. Their achievements reinforce their self-confidence. Past successes make it extremely difficult for them to ask for help when they need it. This is not always due to rebellion; it is usually because of their internalized belief in their ability to fix everything, including themselves. The problem is we are blind to our own self-sabotaging behaviors; consequently, we continually repeat them, which produce cyclical patterns of behavior and results. It is not uncommon to find a high D who has started many businesses that end in the same way. One high D told me, "I have started nine businesses, made them successful, and then lost them one after the other."

- Result-oriented: This decisive, result-oriented, powerful personality will get things done. This strength is valuable in a great leader and is highly rewarded. However, when this strength is carried to excess, D types lose sight of people who may be hurt by their actions; they only see the goal. This blindness is at the heart of the expression "the end justifies the means." Consequently, people are often considered necessary collateral damage. While people generally like working for a result-oriented leader, they often feel used, abused, and abandoned when the task is completed. As a result, the D often alienates employees, friends, and even family members.

- Competitive: The highly competitive nature of the D serves well when winning is the goal. However, the overwhelming need to win often robs this personality type of simply having fun and enjoying life. One high D was overheard saying to his friends during a game of pool, "Let's hurry up with this game so we can start another." I suspect he was losing that game.

  Of all the personality types, this one is the quickest to make decisions and is the most decisive. This strength carried to its extreme may make these individuals blind and deaf to other people's ideas, and they even may become confrontational and intimidating to avoid considering other options.

- Courageous: D types will never be accused of cowardice. Their strength will enable them to try what others can only dream of doing. Their self-confident, competitive, goal-oriented attitude will make them succeed, if there is any way to do so. The problem is the more unhealthy the Ds are, the greater their propensity to ignore risks and endanger themselves and others.

- Direct: The directness and straightforward manner of this personality type is often considered a strong leadership quality. Yet, when taken too far, this attribute becomes a weakness due to the D's harsh tone and brutal bluntness. This ruthless approach often alienates the high D from support systems needed to accomplish the task. This can result in anger, unacknowledged fears, criticism of a perceived lack of loyalty in others, and outrage at the absence of appreciation from society in general.

The High I Personality's Strengths and Weaknesses

- Enthusiastic: The primary strength of this personality is enthusiasm. No other style has the energy and excitement of a highly stimulated I. If it is fun, exciting, and adventuresome, they are on board. Problems arise when
  ◦ it is no longer fun;
  ◦ something more exciting comes along;
  ◦ a plan is needed, because I types never want to plan. Due to a short attention span, they may appear to have some form of attention deficit disorder (ADD). However, this form of ADD cannot be treated with medication.
- Verbal: Although most believe that this personality has great communication skills, unfortunately, that is only half true. This highly influential style is a great talker but not usually a good listener, which is an important aspect of good communication. The ability to talk without a script is certainly a positive attribute; however, when carried to an extreme, it is often an *avoidance behavior* that can sabotage the best efforts of the I personality type.
- Optimistic: Everybody loves an optimist—well, almost everyone. The high C often thinks the I type's optimism is unmerited and shallow, unless it is backed by facts. The energetic I type's optimistic approach to life leads to many adventures, and some of them actually turn out well. However, as you might expect by now, carried too far this

strength becomes a weakness. The overly optimistic high I type will avoid the negatives, believing that enthusiasm can overcome anything, even an empty checking account. Reckless optimism is a self-sabotaging mechanism that keeps high I personalities from the success their optimism assumes they can attain.

- Involved: Involvement is a hallmark of this personality type. "You can count on me" is their mantra, and they will be first to volunteer for anything and everything. I types desire to gain acceptance and approval through volunteering. This willingness to serve, carried to an extreme, causes them to overcommit and overpromise, which makes them underperform. This prompts other personality types to discount their generally persuasive style and view them as superficial or flaky. Their perceived shallowness damages their credibility, and often leaves them sitting on the sidelines, wondering why they cannot get the validation they desire.

- Spontaneous: Now is a keyword for the spontaneous I. The ability to change direction in the middle of a project can be a valuable asset. This behavioral style is generally not married to any project or idea and can change either in an instant. The negative consequence of this attribute occurs when is change direction without considering the outcome or counting the cost. This can result in unfinished business and a loss of trust from others.

- Persuasive: The popular and persuasive I is typically the sales person of the month, quarter, and year. They personify this adage: "They could sell a refrigerator to an Eskimo living in an igloo." Their persuasive powers come from their charm, optimism, and communication skills. When this is carried too far, it can turn into manipulation and the overselling of shoddy products or bad ideas. Discredited again, I types lose the affirmation they seek and believe there is no alternative but to move on to a new set of friends or another job, church, or club.

- Social: I types are social butterflies, continual affirmers, or validators who make everyone feel welcome and as though they belong. This strength becomes a weakness when to feed the needs of his or her soul, the I feels forced to conform to the beliefs and values of others, regardless of their merit. When people with this personality style are healthy, they are capable of loving people for whom they are rather than for how well those people meet their needs.

- Creative: Another strength of this inspiring type is creativity, which flows from a vivid imagination. I types love bright colors; in fact, they often can remember the color of an object better than facts about it. They will give directions using the colors of landmarks rather than street or landmark names. They will remember the color of the shirt you were wearing when they met you but may not recall your name.

- Imaginative: I types have imaginative minds, which are easily distracted. They may go to the store and come back with everything but what they went for. My wife and I went to dinner once at the home of such a friend. The man's wife asked him to run to the store and get something she needed for the meal. He returned three hours later. He ran into friends at the store and forgot why he went and that he had guests in his home. To say he lost touch with reality is an understatement. A highly imaginative mind is a strength, but it becomes a weakness when carried to an extreme. There is help for this, but it does not come in pill form. This personality style has to learn to focus.

The High S Personality Style's Strengths and Weaknesses

- Stable: The healthy high S is resolute and stable. These admirable strengths, although not exclusive to this behavioral style, are a hallmark of it. Yet when this strength is carried to an extreme, the world of the S begins to shrink due to this type's detached patterns of behavior. This stubborn immovability can be problematic to other people in the life of the S personality. For example, an I spouse or D friend can become frustrated and bored by the lack of adventure, engagement, and avoidance of challenges in the relationship.

- Organized: The companion of stability is organization. This steady, even-paced behavioral style can be very organized and methodical. This strength carried to the extreme resists change and refuses to try new things. Resistance looks different in this type. It may not be total rebellion but a passive resistance manifested in disengagement, complacency, and neglectfulness of self and others—in plainer words, pure old-fashioned procrastination.

- Serene: Another apparent strength of this personality is a calm, cool, and collected demeanor. The strength of this behavior is patience and calmness under pressure. When this is taken to the extreme, the S seems to have no initiative or willingness to make decisions. Remember, one of the drives of this style is certainty in relationships. When making a decision appears to threaten a friendship or create any kind of conflict, the default behavior is to disengage, stall, and emotionally disappear.

- Agreeable: Softhearted and agreeable are two positive descriptors of this style. This personality behavior certainly works in favor of the healthy S by disarming the angry, dominant D style, bringing rationality to an overexcited I type, or calmness to any group of people. When this behavior is taken to the extreme, the unhealthy, softhearted, agreeable S can be manipulated and fail to stand up for himself or herself. Such behavior produces a pattern of self-sacrificing in order to please others.

- Attentive: Compared to the other basic personality types, S types have the greatest capacity to be good listeners. However, you cannot always interpret their silence as listening. When this strength becomes unbalanced, what may appear to be good listening skills actually may be the withholding of good ideas or total disengagement from the conversation. One thing to remember is that S types will not compete for an audience; they need time and space in order to give a response and to engage with others.

- Loyal: As we will discover in the next section, S types share the strengths of loyalty and reliability with the C. However, within the S, loyalty looks a little different. When carried to an extreme, S types becomes overly protective of others at their own expense. They will become victims for others to use and abuse. They may cover up the bad behaviors of others. These actions, which appear to be in humility and service, actually may be an unhealthy attempt to meet their own needs.

The High C Personality Style's Strengths and Weaknesses

- Analytical: The primary strength of C types is their analytical skills; details nourish their souls. Other personality styles may like details, but they may lack the drive to seek them out or the patience to wait on the findings of analysis. When carried to an extreme, C types will become overly critical of others and themselves. They often fall into the trap of overanalyzing and become stuck in the decision-making process.

- Cautious: Cautious and intense would be good descriptions of the C personality. Every team needs this person involved in its decision-making process. The high I may throw caution to the wind in favor of popular opinion; high Ds may lack thoughtfulness because they want to follow their gut instincts, but the high C is an influence for rationality. When this strength crosses to the unhealthy side, they tend to withdraw from people and give in to their need to be alone. This is both a rejection of others and of self.

- Aware: A strength of the perfectionist personality is a level of awareness of the environment. C personalities are aware of the feelings of others and the mood of the room. Their level of sensitivity heightens their instinctive knowledge of what others are thinking or feeling. When overused, these strengths cause Cs to become unsettled, concerned about everything, and overly critical of things that do not matter. Unhealthy Cs may become self-absorbed, temperamental, and even secretively self-indulgent. They can crossover from healthy awareness to a form of phobic (neurotic) awareness. This can raise their negative energy level to a point of explosion (manifested outwardly) or implosion (manifested inwardly). Implosion for this type is generally expressed as depression.

- Meticulous: This behavioral pattern's need for excellence and correct procedures and a high set of personal standards brings value to all of our lives. Excellence resonates in the heart and soul of all personality types but not at the same level as it does in the high C. For other types, excellence may be a learned skill, but for C types, it is an instinctive need. With this drive for perfection, their fear of making a mistake may keep them from taking the risks necessary for personal growth and development.

- Loyal: As stated above, the high S shares this valuable trait. However, in the C style, loyalty is lived out in quality relationships. The trust level of this personality behavioral style is low. However, once you earn his or her trust you will have a friend for life. Cs are generally people of their word and love very deeply. When their trust is betrayed, they are wounded deep in their souls.

- Romantic: High Cs are the most romantic of all the personality behavioral styles. They love candlelit dinners, classical music, love stories, and poetry. As stated above, they love cautiously but deeply.

Summary

Strengths carried to an extreme become weaknesses, which are self-sabotaging behaviors. All self-sabotaging behaviors defeat the development of personal or *internal validation,* positive and affirming self-talk. This often creates self-rejection. Self-acceptance is an important and healthy goal. When internal validation, self-acceptance, and approval take place, we can move into a realistic, highly productive, joyful, and satisfying life.

> The thing that is really hard and really amazing is giving up on being perfect and beginning the work of becoming yourself.[6]

Chapter 5

The Stain of Shame

> You have an enemy who wants you stuck in
> your present situation, buried in problems,
> and less successful than you ought to
> be. I am referring to the enemy of your
> soul—*shame.*

At first glance, shame may seem like a detour from the subject of behavioral styles, but let me assure you, it is not. As you will see, shame is one of the greatest obstacles we must overcome to become the people we were created to be.

Shame often is rooted deep within the fabric of the soul and may be the result of well-intended parents. Expressions like "shame on you" and "you ought to be ashamed of yourself" and many more become stains on the self-image of the soul. Shame becomes part of our identities, tainting everything with its mark.

Before we blame everything on our parents, remember that shame was birthed in the Garden of Eden. When Adam and Eve disobeyed, they became aware that they were naked and used fig leaves to cover their shame. That was the first example of humans trying to cover shame.

Shame goes deeper than guilt or failure. It goes to the core of our beings, our souls. We experience shame when our mistakes, either real or perceived, become our identities, and we equate ourselves with those mistakes: "I made a mistake; therefore, I am a mistake."

After speaking at a church on the topic of shame, I received the following letter from a great mom who learned to give her shame a voice:

> Hello Dr. McCray!
>
> Thank you so much for that awesome class last night! During the time, you asked everyone to be quiet and search for areas of shame in their lives, it was revealed that I was ashamed of being a single mother. I was so surprised by that revelation. The thoughts brought me back to the moment I told my parents (separately) that I was pregnant for the first time; I was 18.
>
> My mother immediately began to cry and told me that she wanted better for me. My father said that he was extremely disappointed and didn't speak to me for a year. Other family members responded in a similar way, expressing that I should be embarrassed. My grandmother encouraged me to marry the father to avoid the embarrassment and shame of being single and pregnant. I even remembered times that I resented being a single mom and grieved that my father looked at me the way he did.

Long story short, time has passed, and my oldest son will soon be 15, and my youngest is 11, so it was a surprise for me to realize that I still felt that shame. After it was revealed, I had another revelation. I realized that even now I was reluctant to share with people that I was a single mother and had never been married. The degree of shame I felt resonated to my core. I recognized that I had become so comfortable with my shame that I no longer realized it was there! Needless to say, I am now free and the shame is gone! Thanks again for speaking on this topic. It was so freeing!

What You Need to Know about Shame

- Shame is a universal experience; no person or culture is exempt from the stain of shame. It reaches into the mansions, castles, government halls, and the poorest of homes. It reaches the educated and the so-called uneducated. To avoid shame, people would have to shut off their emotions to avoid the experience of pain.
- Shame thrives in seclusion and avoidance and hides in our silence. No one wants to talk about shame, and no one wants to admit that he or she has shame. It will not yield to silence; shame must be heard before healing can begin. Your pain must be given a therapeutic voice.
- Shame often begins at an early age; we may be shamed by parents and significant people in our lives, which begins the stain of shame in our souls.

- Many children are taught to be ashamed of their bodies and in adolescence are taught to be ashamed of their sexuality. Too often, we were compared to others and if not overtly told to be ashamed, we get the covert message.
- Shame often is created during early teen years when we are outside the "in" group and at many other times.
- Carl Jung referred to shame as the swampland of the soul, a place filled with its own monsters of thoughts, feelings, and words. The language or voice of shame says:

What will people think?

I can't really love myself because I'm . . . not pretty enough, skinny enough, successful enough, rich enough, talented enough, happy enough, feminine enough, masculine enough, sexy enough, productive enough, nice enough, strong enough, tough enough, caring enough, popular enough, creative enough, admired enough, spiritual enough, etc.

Shame is either about being too much or not enough of something. In her book *The Gifts of Imperfection*, author and researcher Brené Brown states,

If we want to know why we're all so afraid to let our true selves be seen and known, we have to understand the power of shame and fear. If we can't stand up to the "never

> good enough" and "who do you think you
> are," we can't move forward.[7]

One client, a forty-year-old junior executive for a large corporation, came to me after he was passed over for a promotion. The quality of his work was not the problem, and he had relatively good people skills for a high D personality. However, he had a problem relating to his boss, who had a patronizing, condescending manner.

I asked him, "How old do you feel when you are in a meeting with your boss?" His response was immediate: "Eight years old. I feel eight years old." I asked what significant thing had happened to him when he was eight. He said that as a child he was so intense when playing that he sometimes forgot to go to the bathroom and would wet his pants. When this occurred, his father would humiliate him by putting a diaper on him, making him stand in front of the family, and revealing how shameful he was. The emotional soul wound this shaming created manifested when he felt humiliated by an authority figure. After processing those destructive emotions from the past, he was able to deal with the present in a more positive way.

The Greatest Enemy of Transformation Is Shame

The goal in overcoming shame is not to cover up the past, but to heal it so that transformation can take place.

Recent research has revealed that every experience and memory not only is deposited in our brain's memory bank, it also is placed into our body's cells.[8] That means every experience we think is shameful has been deposited in our brains and bodies to create stains on our souls. This can even cause our bodies to become diseased.

When we are whole and have been healed of the crippling emotions of our past, we can make choices from healthy mind-sets rather than from wounded and shame-filled frames of mind. Until we are healed, shame powerfully influences our every action and decision.

We often deal with shame by trying to live a perfect life. Often this is simply neurotic perfectionism, which produces a toxic belief system that leads to further shame. By forcing people into false styles of behavior in order to make them acceptable in our spiritual and social clubs, we create within people ideal selves that are unattainable. Acting perfect does not make you perfect; wholeness is an inside job. Shame is like a permanent stain in a carpet; we may think superficial actions erase it, but before long, it reappears.

The woman who came to my office looked much older than her age; she would not look anyone in the eye. She appeared feeble, talked barely above a whisper, and apologized for taking up my time. She had been to several doctors and was on powerful antidepressant and anxiety medications. Now in her third marriage, she was not sure that she would remain in the relationship, even though her husband was good to her.

She reported how verbally abusive and unfaithful her previous husbands had been. She told me how ashamed she was that she could not be good enough to keep those previous relationships together. She even took the blame for her former husbands' infidelity. She was sure that if she had been a better wife, they would not have been so abusive. "I just wasn't good enough," she lamented. Her current husband was bewildered when she said that she knew he wanted to be with other women and that she would not hold him back. He assured me, and tried to assure her, that this was not his desire at all.

As I began dealing with the many issues she perceived as shameful and counseling her about her former husbands' personal responsibility for their actions, things began to change. I will never forget the day she breezed into my office with a spring in her step and a smile on her face; she looked twenty years younger. When I asked, "How are you feeling?" she responded with a smile, "I have never felt better in my life. I feel younger, freer, and happier." There had truly been a transformation; her soul wound had been healed, and her body was responding in kind. She is still going strong and happily married.

Her toxic belief system and shameful self-perception had taken a toll on her emotionally, physically, and relationally. Shame does the same thing to you and me.

Becoming Who You Are

Until we can own our stories of pain and shame, we will never know who we were created to be.

I recently asked a woman of significant accomplishments if she loves who she is. Her answer was, "Yes, in spite of where I came from, I like who I am today." My question sent her on a journey back to her past so she could enjoy her future.

When you celebrate who you are despite your past, you are merely ego or performance driven. However, when you can celebrate who you are because of your past, you are able to live out of your soul and be led by your passions. Your present state of success can never exceed the health of your soul. An unhealthy soul eats away at your accomplishments.

Not being enough keeps us rooted in the shame of our story, which prevents us from owning who we are. Always trying to be somebody that we are not keeps us in a perpetual cycle of shame. Shame whispers in our ear, "If people really know who you are, they will never like you."

A woman who had been in the grip of guilt and shame for most of her life came to me for help. She said okay, then took a deep breath to gather the energy and courage to tell her story. "I need to tell you this, and then I will leave, because I know you won't want to help me once you know what I have done."

She then proceeded to tell she'd had an abortion when she was sixteen. When I did not look shocked or sound alarmed, she told me about five more abortions. Now in middle age, she was so overwhelmed by guilt and shame she was petrified to tell her story to anyone. But she also was compelled to tell someone. When she realized that I would not reject her and that she was in a safe place, I walked her through forgiving herself and her parents who forced her to get the early abortions. Today, she is free from shame and living a productive life with her teenage daughter and loving husband.

Shame shows up in the most familiar places: how we look, the money we have or don't have, etc. I have worked with people who were ashamed of how much money they had, and others who were ashamed because they did not have enough. Shame shows up in our health or the lack of it. What parent has not dealt with shame for mishandling an incident with a child? Unfortunately, there is also the shame brought on by religion—never doing enough good, praying often enough, serving enough, or giving enough. The shame-filled person can never do or be enough.

Regrettably, shame is the controlling force in most religions. In fact, many church cultures are designed to control people rather than empower them to grow and work out their salvation (see Philippians 2:12). This is strange in light of the Gospels' description of Jesus as a friend of the vilest of sinners (see Luke 7:34). The Jesus of the Gospels looks nothing like the perfectionist, condemning Jesus portrayed in most religious circles.

The point is this: true transformation cannot take place in an environment of self-rejection or repressed and unhealed emotional damage. It is not enough merely to know and understand ourselves, even though that is very important.

> More important than *knowing ourselves* and more essential for living a transformed, abundant life is learning how to *love ourselves*. This is the path to becoming the person you have always been but were never allow to be.

Steps to Overcoming Shame

In *The Gifts of Imperfection*, Brown identifies four common denominators shared by men and women who experience recovery from shame:

1. They understand shame and recognize the mental messages and expectations that trigger shame.
2. They practice critical awareness by doing a reality check on any messages or expectations that imply that imperfection equals inadequacy.
3. They reach out and share their stories with people they trust.
4. They speak about shame. They use the word *shame*, talk about how shame makes them feel, and seek relief from it.[9]

Research shows that no part of our culture is equipped to deal with shame: our churches, schools, families, and the corporate world do not know how to deal with this prevailing emotion. Our goal is not to cover up the past; it is to heal the past so we can take ownership of that part of ourselves. Then, and only then, can transformation take place.

At the beginning of this chapter, I mentioned that shame originated in the Garden of Eden. When Adam and Eve disobeyed God, they tried to cover their shame with leaves. However, when God came on the scene, he gave them coverings of animal hides, symbolizing that human efforts to deal with shame were inadequate, and one who was innocent would be slain for their sins and bear their shame. The Messiah would not merely cover but would remove their stains of shame. Consequently, anyone can become free of shame.

Section 2

Chapter 6

Hindrances to Living
in the Present

> Much of what we were at five or six is what
> we wind up wishing we could be at fifty
> or sixty.[10]

When we first discover personality styles, we see them primarily as mirrors reflecting our images and the images of others. However, after years of study and thousands of hours spent counseling people, I am convinced it is something far more. The material presented in this book is a tool that can unlock the hidden potential many people believe resides within them but they are unable to release.

The life-impacting process of becoming present will give you the tools to stop reinforcing habitual negative personality patterns and make a conscious decision for transformation. This is scientifically known as transcribing neuroplasticity, but the rest of us know it as renewing the mind or remapping the brain.

Learning to Be Present

In the previous section, you gained a basic understanding of how you view the world and how the world views you, which is important in your relationship to yourself (intrapersonal) and to others (interpersonal). The goals of this section are to:

1. Help you become awakened to habitually destructive patterns that sabotage your best intentions and keep the real you buried under the toxic trio of self-punishment, self-rejection, and self-devaluation.
2. Demonstrate ways to defuse and heal unconscious, negative childhood messages that have a detrimental impact on your present reality.
3. Learn to identify and work with the motivators in your life, the values and beliefs that drive behavior. You cannot change a behavior without changing the belief and value that drive that unwanted, destructive pattern.
4. Discover how to use the understanding of personality types for continual growth and development—personally, professionally, and relationally.

Preoccupations of the Personality Types:

The following adaptation of behavioral styles from Helen Palmer, author of *Enneagram: Understanding Yourself and the Others in Your Life*, helps us identify some of the unconscious thinking patterns of each personality type.[11]

The Preoccupations of the High D

The unhealthy high D will use control as a way to avoid dealing with or living in the present. Ds will become preoccupied with things, possessions, and space. They may get busy arranging and rearranging things like furniture, the garage, books shelves, cabinets, the sock drawer, etc.

They may try to find relief from current stressful situations by controlling people. They can become aggressive and display anger by destroying property, hurting others, or hurting themselves. They use this behavior to make people afraid to approach them about any pressing issues.

Another behavior, which on the surface looks very admirable, is fighting for justice and the protection of others. In the preoccupation state, issues that may not have been important to them before now consume their attention.

Unhealthy high Ds will become excessive in their actions and reactions to avoid the boredom of living in the present. They may keep late hours, entertain themselves excessively, or binge on everything from food to exercise. A high D personality type told me he would get two or three part-time jobs to avoid depression or loneliness.

The independent nature of high Ds will cause them to go to great lengths and sometimes do foolish things just to prove that they do not need other people. This behavior to avoid being present is disguised as self-sufficiency.

The pathway out of this unconscious pattern of behavior is to become self-aware. I often refer to this as "catching yourself in the act." The following questions awaken us from our default patterns of behavior. To assist the reader, I will list these questions after each personality behavioral style.

- Is my current behavior positive or negative?
- What emotion or emotions do I feel at the moment?
- What event or events are triggering these emotions or thought processes?
- Is my response appropriate to the current situation?
- If not, what past event may be triggering this response?

- Is my behavior having a positive or negative effect on other people?
- When do I feel most vulnerable?
- How do I behave when I feel vulnerable?
- How does this affect my relationships?
- How does this affect my job performance?
- Is there a pattern of behavior I would like to change?
- If I were to change one negative behavior, what benefit would that produce personally, professionally, and relationally?
- If I don't change a negative behavior, what will the result be?

The Preoccupations of the High I

The high I personality's struggle to avoid the present is wrapped up in *doing* rather than *being*. High I types will seek and maintain high levels of excitement—going from party to party, from one meeting to the next, and overscheduling themselves to avoid living in the moment. Their classic avoidance behavior includes not opening the mail or not balancing the checkbook, because it would mean facing a current reality. It is more fun to stay busy and fantasize that the bills will go away.

High I types need to stay emotionally high. Therefore, they try to avoid anything that might cause feelings of loneliness, sadness, anxiety, or any other negative emotions. To remain emotionally high, they avoid unpleasant emotions by talking excessively; being overly needy; clinging to friends; overspending; overeating; engaging in lots of sex, drugs, drinking, and partying; and over-spiritualizing.

Another method the high I will use to avoid living in the present is to maintain multiple options as a way to buffer commitment to a single course of action. The high I likes to use exit language, such as, "I will try," "if I can," or "if I have the time." These kinds of statements provide a way to escape being in the present. The following questions are designed to awaken you from destructive patterns of behavior.

- Is my current behavior positive or negative?
- What emotion or emotions do I feel at the moment?
- What event or events are triggering these emotions or thought processes?
- Is my response appropriate to the current situation?
- If not, what past event may be triggering this response?
- Is my behavior having a positive or negative effect on other people?
- When do I feel most vulnerable?
- How do I behave when I feel vulnerable?
- How does this affect my relationships?
- How does this affect my job performance?
- Is there a pattern of behavior I would like to change?
- If I were to change one negative behavior, what benefit would that produce personally, professionally, and relationally?
- If I don't change a negative behavior, what will the result be?

Preoccupations of the High S

The high S personality is quite different from the D or the I. S types will replace the important needs in their lives with less important ones, telling themselves they will do the more essential things at the end of the day. They avoid doing things that will bring them into the present by excessively resting, sleeping, watching TV, surfing the Internet, or playing video games.

High S types avoid making troubling decisions by procrastinating or making decisions that are less consequential. Agreeing or disagreeing is replaced by a passive condition: they leave the interpretation of their behavior to someone else, secretly hoping the other person will discern their true feelings correctly.

Another way they avoid the present is by depending on habitual behaviors and repeating familiar solutions, which become ritualistic.

High S types use procrastination to avoid confrontation or the need to say no, which is another way to avoid living in the present. This often results in the internalization of anger and further avoidance behaviors, which drain their already low energy supply. They then take steps to manage their physical energy by strategically planning their time and commitments, which is merely another avoidance behavior. Ponder the questions below to discover other avoidant patterns of behavior.

- Is my current behavior positive or negative?
- What emotion or emotions do I feel at the moment?
- What event or events are triggering these emotions or thought processes?
- Is my response appropriate to the current situation?
- If not, what past event may be triggering this response?

- Is my behavior having a positive or negative effect on other people?
- When do I feel most vulnerable?
- How do I behave when I feel vulnerable?
- How does this affect my relationships?
- How does this affect my job performance?
- Is there a pattern of behavior I would like to change?
- If I were to change one negative behavior, what benefit would that produce personally, professionally, and relationally?
- If I don't change a negative behavior, what will the result be?

Preoccupations of the High C

The introspective high C brings a completely different dynamic to evasion of the present. These personality types often have an inner feeling that something is missing from their lives and that others have what they are missing. Therefore, they tend to live through others and avoid their own responsibilities. The fear of failure, past disappointments, and the belief that life is too hard, complicated, or unrewarding keeps the C stuck in behavior that avoids living in the present.

Another method of distraction used by the high C is the idealization of an absent lover. This is a push/pull syndrome. People always look better from afar, and the C projects an ideal image on absent friends or lovers. When people show themselves to be less than the unrealistic ideal, the C tends to push them away rather than live with the reality.

As we learned earlier, high Cs control by using their moods as shields to keep people out of their emotional spaces, another way to avoid living in the present. They will develop a mood of gloom or sadness to gain the understanding and sympathy from others rather than be forthright concerning their feelings and emotions. This often leaves the C with a sense of abandonment and loss. This negative emotion may become exaggerated when they engage in other people's traumatic events, such as illness, death, loss, etc. However, this is just another device, and their real intention is to avoid living in the present. Contemplate the following questions to find avoidant behaviors that keep you from living in the present.

- Is my current behavior positive or negative?
- What emotion or emotions do I feel at the moment?
- What event or events are triggering these emotions or thought processes?
- Is my response appropriate to the current situation?
- If not, what past event may be triggering this response?
- Is my behavior having a positive or negative effect on other people?
- When do I feel most vulnerable?
- How do I behave when I feel vulnerable?
- How does this affect my relationships?
- How does this affect my job performance?
- Is there a pattern of behavior I would like to change?
- If I were to change one negative behavior, what benefit would that produce personally, professionally, and relationally?
- If I don't change a negative behavior, what will the result be?

Preoccupations of the Natural Combinations

In this section, we will begin to examine the preoccupations of the personality type combinations. While some of their behaviors will sound familiar, there are some notable differences. For your convenience, I will continue to list the questions at the end of each style's combinations,

Preoccupations of the C/S

The first preoccupation of the C/S combination is the avoidance of involvement. C/S types are observers of life rather than participants in it. Their fear of living in the present is due to the fear of being vulnerable by having to be in touch with their emotions or feelings. They fear this will lead to a loss of their much-treasured privacy.

This combination maintains a personality of self-control by detaching attention from feelings and excessively compartmentalizing his or her life. C/S types will keep each commitment in a separate box, with a time limit on each obligation. They want predictability rather than variability, which to them means vulnerability.

A major type of avoidance is viewing life and oneself from an outsider's point of view, even to the extent of referring to oneself in the third person (i.e., he or she). This allusion of self-control provides the C/S the ability to avoid living in the here and now. The result of this kind of control is a delayed emotional response to current situations. C/S combinations only allow their emotions to surface when they are alone in safe places. As you consider these questions from the combinations you may discover more roadblocks to living in the present.

- Is my current behavior positive or negative?
- What emotion or emotions do I feel at the moment?
- What event or events are triggering these emotions or thought processes?
- Is my response appropriate to the current situation?
- If not, what past event may be triggering this response?
- Is my behavior having a positive or negative effect on other people?
- When do I feel most vulnerable?
- How do I behave when I feel vulnerable?
- How does this affect my relationships?
- How does this affect my job performance?
- Is there a pattern of behavior I would like to change?
- If I were to change one negative behavior, what benefit would that produce personally, professionally, and relationally?
- If I don't change a negative behavior, what will the result be?

Preoccupations of the I/D

As discussed in an earlier chapter, the I/D has a need to be significant. I types have a need for recognition, and the D needs recognition for accomplishments. When combined, the I/D's need for recognition results in a preoccupation with achievements and performance. This combination believes love results from what you do and from prestige, rather than from who you are. I/Ds want to be identified with successful and popular people and often claim success for things they had little or nothing to do with. I/Ds become so externally focused that they have no time or attention remaining for the present.

This personality type focuses on efficiency and competency at the expense of being real or genuine, both of which are characteristic of living in the present. Their focus can be so strong, I/D types will be unaware of their physical or emotional pain until the job is finished. Consequently, the avoidance of being in the present often leads them to abuse their bodies and emotions.

As an I/D personality type, I can attest to this fact. Sometimes my wife will ask, "Are you feeling okay?" Generally, I reply, "Sure. Why?" Then after a task is completed, I will notice that I do not feel well. I have worked with a number of high D and I/D men who have abused their bodies and chalked it up to hard work. They ignore their pain and everything else in the present, because they have no time for those distractions while completing a task.

Unaware I/Ds need to present an image they believe will gain approval. This preoccupation leads to confusion between the real self in the present and the characteristics the I/D perceives as appropriate for the job or to gain the desired acceptance.

I/Ds generally have good work ethics and do not feel that anyone owes them a living. However, when this strength is carried to the extreme, they will not always take the time to build relationships and seek the help they need. To do so requires living in the moment and being in touch with current reality. They fear that doing so may show that they are different from the image they are trying to project.

The fear of being found out keeps them on an emotional treadmill, racing to stay one step ahead of whom they really are. They accomplish this by talking about superficial things, like their present tasks, jobs, careers, and projects, rather than by promoting intimacy with talk about their feelings, relationships, and emotions.

I recently worked with a high I/D personality who was so caught up in identifying with a so-called mentor that he lost his own identity. He lived in conflict because he failed to recognize the value of his true self and personal potential. He could not sleep and had been diagnosed with an autoimmune disease. (Autoimmunity is the failure of an organism to recognize its own constituent parts as belonging to itself. Hence, it creates an immune response against its own cells and tissues.) My goal was to help him find his own identity and unlock his potential.

> When I/Ds learn to live in the present, they can find their own passion, purpose, and destiny instead of trying to live in the destiny of others.

- Is my current behavior positive or negative?
- What emotion or emotions do I feel at the moment?
- What event or events are triggering these emotions or thought processes?
- Is my response appropriate to the current situation?
- If not, what past event may be triggering this response?
- Is my behavior having a positive or negative effect on other people?
- When do I feel most vulnerable?

- How do I behave when I feel vulnerable?
- How does this affect my relationships?
- How does this affect my job performance?
- Is there a pattern of behavior I would like to change?
- If I were to change one negative behavior, what benefit would that produce personally, professionally, and relationally?
- If I don't change a negative behavior, what will the result be?

Preoccupations of the I/S

You may remember that the I side of any personality combination needs approval and acceptance. When you add in the S type, the preoccupations take on interesting variations.

The S side avoids confrontations in the interest of keeping relationships. In the I/S combination that manifests as the need to make other people dependent, with the attitude, *They will never make it with without me.* I/S types take pride in meeting the needs of others, believing, *I don't need anyone, but they all need me.* Consequently, they tend to serve others rather than acknowledge their own needs. Their empathic connection with other people's feelings and their adaptability to the wishes of others is a manipulative way of assuring that they are loved, which is a way to avoid living in the present.

I/S types' continuous preoccupation to serve others produces confusion, because they develop many identities to meet the needs of various people. Living through others eventually gives them feelings of resentment and the belief they are being controlled by other people's needs. Fearing that people will stop liking them if they stop being overly generous and supportive, they settle for this imitation of life. They may also develop a romantic attachment to the "great" man or the "inspiring" woman they serve. The challenge to living in the present for I/S types is to separate their identities from those of the people they serve and attend to their own needs. Continue to focus on the questions for insight into living in the present.

- Is my current behavior positive or negative?
- What emotion or emotions do I feel at the moment?
- What event or events are triggering these emotions or thought processes?
- Is my response appropriate to the current situation?
- If not, what past event may be triggering this response?
- Is my behavior having a positive or negative effect on other people?
- When do I feel most vulnerable?
- How do I behave when I feel vulnerable?
- How does this affect my relationships?
- How does this affect my job performance?
- Is there a pattern of behavior I would like to change?
- If I were to change one negative behavior, what benefit would that produce personally, professionally, and relationally?
- If I don't change a negative behavior, what will the result be?

Preoccupations of the C/D

The powerful combination of the C/D styles comes with great strengths; the intuitiveness of the D and the analytical side of the C usually gives this personality an edge in the business world.

The challenge for C/Ds lies in their need for correctness, which produces a habitual stream of self-criticizing thoughts, complicated by a compulsive need to act on what seems to be correct. The constant need to compare themselves to others combined with their concern about criticism hinders them from living in the here and now.

When C/Ds fear making a mistake, even as they see the potential for perfection, they become caught in a vicious cycle of avoidance and over analyzing. The decision-making process comes to a grinding halt. This tug-of-war keeps C/D personalities from living in the present for fear they might miss a better alternative.

C/D personalities can become so preoccupied with unmet needs and the fear of making mistakes that they transfer their anger to others who may be innocent. Alternatively, they may internalize their anger and escape the present through depression or by taking on additional projects. This type of behavior can lead to the emergence of two selves: (1) the worried self who hides at home in a depressed state, or (2) a playful self who acts out in unusual ways when away from home. Either state is merely a way to avoid being present. Again, use the questions to raise your level of consciousness.

- Is my current behavior positive or negative?

- What emotion or emotions do I feel at the moment?
- What event or events are triggering these emotions or thought processes?
- Is my response appropriate to the current situation?
- If not, what past event may be triggering this response?
- Is my behavior having a positive or negative effect on other people?
- When do I feel most vulnerable?
- How do I behave when I feel vulnerable?
- How does this affect my relationships?
- How does this affect my job performance?
- Is there a pattern of behavior I would like to change?
- If I were to change one negative behavior, what benefit would that produce personally, professionally, and relationally?
- If I don't change a negative behavior, what will the result be?

Conclusion

We must push the envelope to find wholeness, passion, and purpose by living in the present instead of following our preprogrammed reactions. When we do this, it is normal to feel anxious, and sense that something is out of kilter and pushing us beyond our comfort zone. At this point, we should be encouraged, because allowing ourselves to experience some anxiety is the beginning of the transformational process. Don't let those feelings put you off; they are a good thing, because chaos always precedes transformation.

To be present means to become fully awake, conscious, and aware of the habitual responses and attitudes that keep us from living in the present. Reactive responses and attitudes are merely habits of thought, tied to emotions that must yield to our determination to change.

Chapter 7

Learning to Live in the Present

> The quality of the self-conscious mind endows organisms with one of the most powerful forces in the Universe—the opportunity to express free will.[12]

The more aware we are of the attitudes and motives that underlie our behavior, the more present we become. Most of our reactions are automatic because they are governed by unconscious impulses based on values and beliefs we internalized at a very young age. While they may have been appropriate in childhood, they often prove to be detrimental in adulthood. Although we are not always able to learn the full extent of what drives our behavior, by recognizing the stimulants that drive us, we can make better choices.

At this point, you may have caught a glimpse of your innate and learned behaviors and habits; many of them originated in past generations and were handed down to you through your ancestors. Living in the present is the beginning of transformation, and the fundamental technique for finding your way to the present is developing self-awareness. Self-awareness is different from self-consciousness.

The personality profiles are a way to become self-aware and begin the process of transformation. The risk of learning about our personality styles is that we may use them as excuses for negative behavior, which can result when we have too much information without experiencing transformation.

Such a person might say, "Well, I am this way because of my personality, so you will just have to live with it." Obviously, this attitude can never produce growth or unlock one's potential.

Habitual patterns of thought require little or no reasoning or self-awareness, and keep us in patterns of repetitive behavior that produce the same negative results over and over again. I have worked with people who build businesses that fail; then they build again, and fail again. Obviously, there is an unconscious, self-sabotaging behavior driven by a negative belief system that keeps this pattern recycling. People do this not only in business but in relationships, addictions, sicknesses/health, weight loss/gain, and on and on.

We have to learn how to break out of old patterns before we can breakthrough to new dimensions.

Catch Yourself in the Act

Learning to catch yourself in the act of a dysfunctional behavior or a counterproductive thought process is the beginning of transformational work. The questions from the last chapter will help you identify the areas for growth. You cannot change what you are unaware of or what you will not own. If you do not own and value your past, you become blinded by it and constantly run away from it.

> If you are blinded by your past, you cannot see your future, and if you are running from your past, you cannot step into your potential.

Catching yourself in the act means becoming aware of negative behaviors, thoughts, and attitudes that sabotage your personal goals, relationships, and career. When we are unaware of the triggers or stimulants that set these behaviors in motion, our emotions highjack us, and we go down familiar but destructive pathways. We will discuss the various ways this is experienced in the chapter about ego boundaries. Most life coaches agree that if negative influences are not neutralized within an hour, they can wreck your day, week, month, and sometimes the rest of your life.

Owning or honoring your past does not mean that you *like* what happened to you or what you may have done to others. It is merely facing the reality of the past and removing its guilt, shame, judgments, and condemnation by forgiving others and yourself. It may appear to be easier to forgive others than it is to forgive yourself; however, that is a false forgiveness at best and will generally come back to hurt you in some way. We cannot effectively do for others what we cannot do for ourselves.

To allow oneself to continue to be hooked by guilt is also a way of avoiding responsibility and living in the present. One client told me she felt like she had fishhooks all over her body. Her analogy was very accurate. She had a number of incidents for which she needed to forgive herself. In other words, she needed to let herself off the hook.

> What happened to you may not have been your fault; however, that does not change the fact that your healing and your spiritual and personal growth are your responsibility; no one can do this for you.

When we remove the negatives of guilt, shame, judgment, and condemnation from our pasts, we can discover who we are today. In addition, we find out who we have the potential to become—not in spite of our past but because of it. This is a part of the meaning of "all things work together for the good of those called according to His purpose" (Romans 8:28 KJV). To put it another way, "We know that in all things God works for the good of those who love him. He appointed them to be saved in keeping with his purpose" (Romans 8:28 NIRV).

The most effective way for dealing with the shame, guilt, and condemnation that are rooted in our fallen natures is through the atoning price Jesus paid for the sins of the world.

> He took the punishment, and that made us whole. Through his bruises we get healed. We're all like sheep who've wandered off and gotten lost. We've all done our own thing, gone our own way. And God has piled all our sins, everything we've done wrong, on him. (Isaiah 53:6 MSG)

When we accept the transfer of shame, guilt, judgment, and condemnation from us to Christ by acknowledging him as our Savior, our sins are forgiven. We are released from the negative things that keep us from being our true selves: "because if you confess with your lips that Jesus is Lord and believe in your heart that God raised him from the dead, you will be saved. For one believes with the heart and so is justified, and one confesses with the mouth and so is saved" (Romans 10:9–10 NRSV).

That is the good news of the Gospel. Unfortunately, this is not always the message that is communicated by many religious cultures. They often present a different view of Christ's atonement than what we find in the New Testament. Consequently, Christianity can become nothing more than an ego-driven, performance-based set of rules and regulations rather than a life-challenging and life-changing relationship with our Creator.

The work of Christ on the cross is the only basis for true transformation without condemnation: "Therefore, [there is] now no condemnation (no adjudging guilty of wrong) for those who are in Christ Jesus, who live [and] walk not after the dictates of the flesh, but after the dictates of the Spirit" (Romans 8:1 AMP). Notice the wording of this verse: "Walk not after the *dictates of the flesh*, but after the *dictates of the Spirit*" (italics added).

Within each of us, a negative, condemning voice judges our every thought and behavior against an ideal self that exists below our conscious thought. We begin developing this unrealistic model of correct performance the day we come into the world. The ideal self is just that—an *ideal*. Still, it is the person we think we ought to be or should have become. It produces in us a less-than syndrome because our actual performance can never measure up to the perfection of the ideal self.

The problem with the ideal self is that it is rooted in legalism and self-judgment based on strict adherence to precise rules. Even if we come close to attaining that ideal, we immediately will raise the bar higher to make the standard impossible to reach. The image of the ideal self is false, but it speaks with a deafening voice in our conscious minds.

Dictates of the Unredeemed Ego Driven by the Ideal Self

The language of the super ego—the part of us that is filled with judgment and conditional love—is "should have," "shouldn't have," "could have," "ought to," etc. It is always speaking judgment, condemnation, shame, and guilt, and the final result is self-punishment, self-rejection, and loss of personal esteem or value.

The language of the id—the flesh where our innate desires, such as hunger, thirst, and the need for relationships, love, and acceptance, reside—is "if it feels good, do it." Living out this maxim leaves you in a state of regret and emptiness. Not every impulse has to be acted on but neither does it have to be judged.

The language of the ego or mind is "I am in charge; I create my own destiny; I am my own god." Living this way leads to disappointment and the endless redoubling of efforts to meet personal expectations. The dictates of the ideal self are always negative, and they produce a corrective self that continually goads us into trying to raise the level of our performance.

Disappointing the ideal self calls forth an attack by the toxic trio of self-punishment, self-rejection, and disesteem.

This punishment phase causes behavior against others, oneself, or both. Punishment, however, is never about correcting, training, nurturing, or discipline; it is an act of retribution that never changes behavior. It actually reinforces unwanted or negative behavior through overt or covert conduct. It often results in self-sabotage and can even lead to self-destruction.

Each component of the toxic trio of self-punishment, self-rejection, and disesteem looks different in the various personality styles.

Negative Self-Correction of the High D

The D inflicts self-punishment by overworking, exercising excessively, and other extreme behaviors. Unfortunately, these behaviors are rewarded and admired in our culture. Only when there is a crisis of health do we look back and realize the person was acting irresponsibly.

Self-punishing high Ds may hurt themselves. On other occasions, their anger, fueled by their own unacceptable behavior, may manifest as self-glorification, domination, and intimidation. They can become ruthless, dictatorial, and destructive. A young high D man I know sometimes became angry and disappointed in himself. On more than one occasion, he took a baseball bat to his car, smashing windows, headlights, and taillights. When he came to his senses, he would say in bewilderment, "I don't know what came over me." This is an example of an extreme emotional hijacking.

The second component of the negative corrective self is rejection of self and others. This is especially true of high D personality types. They can become cruel to their own bodies.

I worked with a middle-aged male whose body was so broken due to self-punishing acts, he was almost incapacitated, although he looked strong and healthy. You did not have to go far below the surface to discover that he was driven by anger. He stated emphatically, "I have never lived up to my potential." He felt rejected by his father, friends, and other family members and existed in a hell of self-rejection and self-punishment.

He worked harder and longer than his peers; his boss loved him for that and for his willingness to take on projects so difficult no one else would attempt them. He would manually lift things that others would use power equipment to raise. He would jump from heights where others would use a ladder. He was like Superman on the job.

As you would suspect, after years of personal rejection and self-abuse, he required knee replacements and spinal fusion, and a long list of other physical issues had taken their toll. Yet from his viewpoint, he was far from reaching his ideal self. In fact, he was obviously in a state of deterioration, physically and emotionally.

The third component of this destructive trio of negative self-correction is disesteem, which occurs when one compares oneself to others and to one's ideal self, and always comes up short. Disesteem often is the result of being compared to other children by parents and caregivers at an early age. Examples include: "Why can't you be like your brother/sister?" and "You need to be like the other kids; see how good they are?" This kind of comparison is different from the natural competition in which children engage. It comes with a "shame on you" tone that slices deep into the soul of a child, sending the message, "You are a loser." Such comparisons lead to feelings of shame and fundamental inadequacy, but healthy competition builds skills and character.

High D types generally deal with disesteem by overcompensating. They may use boastful, self-glorifying, intimidating, or terrorizing tactics to devalue others so they can feel better about themselves.

I was recently in a class with a high D man, who thought that he should be teaching the class instead of the instructor. His first attempt to elevate himself was by association. He announced that he had the same degrees as the instructor, which was not true. Then he tried to dominate the class by talking over everyone else. When confronted with his behavior, he assured the instructor that he knew more than anyone else in the class and was only there to fulfill a requirement for a position he wanted. Finally, his behavior became so disruptive he had to be removed. Needless to say, that did not go over well with him. Several months later, however, he contacted the professor and apologized for his behavior, which is rare for a high D and indicative of healthy growth.

Negative Self-Correction of the High I

Self-punishment in the high I may take the form of excessive spending, overeating, binging, anorexia, or other reckless behaviors.

Rejection by high I types may result in psychosomatic illness, promiscuity, excessive partying, and trying to prove they belong and are loved.

Remember, the I personality is wired for acceptance, so self-rejection is a serious and dangerous state of mind. I know high I types who suffer from autoimmune diseases, which is often the result of self-hatred and self-rejection.[13]

Disesteem among high I types may make them feel that they have ruined their lives and have no hope for recovery. This belief may produce hysterical activity. They may escape into drugs, alcohol, or other destructive behaviors to avoid comparing themselves to others.

Negative Self-Correction of the High S

Self-punishment of the high S takes various forms; it can manifest as excessive serving to the point of total loss of self or isolating oneself from others. Since high S types tend to fade into the background, their self-punishment is not always obvious.

Self-punishing high S types lose themselves in the crowd. One client told me that she was tired of being a wallflower. This is typical behavior for a self-disappointing S personality type. Self-punishment caused her to take on a "poor me" attitude.

Self-rejection may cause high S types to lose themselves in comforting routines and habits, puttering around or doing anything that will allow them to tune out their problems. Some become so withdrawn into themselves that eventually they are completely unresponsive.

The disesteem of high S types often manifests as an attempt to eliminate their awareness of the here and now. They may try to preserve the illusion of peace by fragmenting themselves into sub-personalities while trudging through life and seeming to hang on by mere wishful thinking, yet all the while suppressing their anger.

Disesteemed high S types may neglect themselves to such an extent, they refuse to eat properly, if at all. They may lose the drive for personal hygiene and stop bathing, changing clothes, or maintaining their environment.

Negative Self-Correction of the High C

High Cs use self-punishment to escape into depression, apathy, constant fatigue, and illness. They become aloof, self-conscious, and melancholy, hoping that their obvious fragility will attract a rescuer.

Their rejection of self and others pushes people away. Although high Cs hope that a knight in shining armor will rescue them from their predicament, they may shoot (i.e., reject or discredit) their rescuer upon arrival. This push/pull behavior leaves high Cs feeling as if they are missing out on life.

Disesteem leaves high C types with self-hatred and distain for those they believe failed to rescue them. They may even attempt to elicit rescue through self-destructive behavior.

One high C client experiencing this destructive corrective style was so filled with self-hatred that she suffered from several debilitating conditions, including respiratory issues, autoimmune conditions, and joint problems. Anger and rejection of self had crippled her. Her disdain for others had isolated her from people who loved her; they were shut out by her negative behavior and attitude.

A moment of self-compassion can change
your entire day. A string of such moments
can change the course of your life.[14]

Those who discover their identity in Christ can face the
past and the present without condemnation, and let go of
the false idol of the ideal self to become the people they were
created to be.

Find hope from these beautiful words of the psalmist:

> Oh yes, you shaped me first inside, then
> out; you formed me in my mother's womb. I
> thank you, High God—you're breathtaking!
> Body and soul, I am marvelously made! I
> worship in adoration—what a creation! You
> know me inside and out, you know every
> bone in my body; You know exactly how
> I was made, bit by bit, how I was sculpted
> from nothing into something. Like an
> open book, you watched me grow from
> conception to birth; all the stages of my
> life were spread out before you, *the days of
> my life all prepared before I'd even lived one
> day*. (Psalm 139:13–16 MSG; italics added)

The prophet Jeremiah wrote:

> . . . I have it all planned out—plans to
> take care of you, not abandon you, plans
> to give you the future you hope for. When
> you call on me, when you come and pray
> to me, I'll listen. When you come looking

for me, you'll find me. Yes, when you get serious about finding me and want it more than anything else, I'll make sure you won't be disappointed. God's Decree. "I'll turn things around for you." (Jeremiah 29:13, 14 MSG)

The apostle Paul states:

It's in Christ that we find out who we are and what we are living for. Long before we first heard of Christ and got our hopes up, he had his eye on us, had designs on us for glorious living, part of the overall purpose he is working out in everything and everyone. (Ephesians 1:11–12)

Finding the Real You through Your Passions, Purpose, Desires, Points of Resistance, and Innate Talents

Some important questions to consider:

- Do you feel that your life is not complete?
- Do you believe something is missing?
- Do you wonder how you got here?
- Do you question what you are supposed to do now that you are here?
- Do you suspect that your life is on autopilot and you do not know where you are going?

There is evidence that we come into this world with a purpose and destiny indelibly written into our genes. However, the world system we live in does not agree with that point of view. To accept this truth is to acknowledge there is a Creator and that he is personally involved in our lives. To admit such a view requires believing that we are not accidents or random products of genetics, regardless of the nature of our conception. There is a part of the divine in each of us, because God created us in his image and for his purpose. The deepest longing of the soul is to discover our purpose and begin the journey to our destiny.

I am reminded of the tragic death of professional golfer and pilot, Payne Stewart on October 25, 1999, when his Learjet crashed in South Dakota. The accident investigators concluded that the plane suffered a quick loss of cabin pressure, and all on board died of hypoxia. The pilots' delay of only a few seconds in donning their oxygen masks, coupled with cognitive and motor skill impairment due to a lack of oxygen, could have caused their incapacitation, resulting in the loss of all onboard. The plane, filled with dead and dying people, flew on autopilot until it ran out of fuel.

> Many people live their lives in a state of unconsciousness. Living on autopilot, they are guided by a negative, outdated subconscious belief system that may be steering them to spiritual and physical death.

What Rocks Your World?

The more we become aware, conscious, or awake to life, the more we can walk in the fullness of God's purpose for our existence. The more we live in the present, the more we become aware of the parts of ourselves that are not at peace with the current moment.

Self-awareness or living in the present breaks into our daydreams and preprogrammed perceptions, yet because of our unconscious preoccupations and other defense mechanisms, we cannot hold on to and remain in the present.

These moments of being alive have a profound place in our memories. They are more vivid and have a greater impact than other memories do. This is because they are connected to our purpose, our calling, and the nature of God within us.

Liz, a young actress, attended one of my classes and shared a moment from her past when she felt most alive. "I was . . . awake to all my senses—feeling, seeing, hearing, tasting, even smelling the atmosphere. It was so powerful that it was frightening."

Such experiences are in the here and now, in the present. Life-impacting moments are powerful because they penetrate the dullness of the consciousness and awaken us. Unless we integrate these experiences into our daily lives, they remain nothing more than vague memories. Their integration requires moving beyond or letting go of one's fear, resistance, and self-image.

Liz presented herself as a quiet, withdrawn, and shy, little girl in a woman's body. As she recounted her experience, she was bold, powerful, and awake to the present. When asked which of those personifications she liked the most, she replied in a small, squeaky voice, "The powerful me scares me."

The more we operate in our conditioned egos, the less we are aware and the more we function through our subconscious values and beliefs. Consequently, we return to the more comfortable at-home feeling of our flesh and become less attentive to the presence of the Holy Spirit in our lives.

Finding our purpose often is perceived to be something mystical, super-spiritual, or outside ourselves, an external manifestation of God's presence. While such expressions of God do occur, they are not the measure of personal growth and development. Since purpose and identity are so closely tied together, it follows that we should look for our identities on the inside rather than the outside.

Barbara, a grandmother, was looking for her purpose and was surprised to discover that it was in the sphere of her family. She was most aware of her physical presence when she was cooking and teaching her grandchildren how to cook. She had never considered that this could be God's purpose for her at this time in her life. After all, that is not the focus of most motivational seminars or goal-setting workshops.

As the class discussed how this might be her purpose, the energy in the room began to escalate. Someone pointed out that teaching children to cook instructs them in discipline, following instructions, and the importance of being connected to the here-and-now touch, smells, tastes, sights, and sounds of the kitchen. This seemingly simple activity was giving her grandchildren valuable life lessons that could not be learned in other settings. Barbara left the class feeling fully alive, validated, and purposeful.

Steps to Finding Your Purpose

Discovering God's purpose is not something to be put off for the future; it is in the present, the here and now. Put another way: "So here's what I want you to do, God helping you: Take your everyday, ordinary life—your sleeping, eating, going-to-work, and walking-around life—and place it before God as an offering. Embracing what God does for you is the best thing you can do for him" (Romans 12:1 MSG).

If we practice the work of this passage, we will realize that these moments of passion, being fully alive or awake, are not extraordinary; they are intended to be a part of everyday life. We must come to understand that such experiences are glimpses into reality, windows to our purpose and destiny. As we mature in our walk with God, we discover that the ordinary is actually extraordinary. Then we can stop chasing some external supernatural experience and live out of the supernatural within us.

Consider these questions to gain insight and find God's purpose for your life:

1. When do you feel most alive?
2. What attracts people to you, causes them to come to you?
3. What interests you the most? Which books, scriptures, etc.?
4. When do you have the most energy?
5. What activity causes you to lose track of time?
6. What could you do forever?
7. What are you hanging onto for no apparent reason?

Instead of forcing yourself to be like someone that you are not, focus on being who you are, but were never allowed to be. As you practice this, you will step into your purpose, your true nature will be unlocked, and you will experience a great transformation.

Chapter 8

Change Your Story and Change Your Life

> When you are fixated on the pains of the past,
> you are blinded to the power of the present.

Being dominated by past pains and events robs us of our present and our future. It is common for people to hide in their past pain and suffering. Their stories are composed of complaints, tension, conflicts, blaming, drama, rationalizations, projections, and self-justifications.

If you believe that problems from your past might be affecting your today, answering the following question can awaken you to the present: if my suffering and everything that surrounds it were to go away, who would I be?

This was the essence of the question Jesus asked a crippled man:

> Soon another Feast came around and Jesus was back in Jerusalem. Near the Sheep Gate in Jerusalem, there was a pool, in Hebrew called Bethesda, with five alcoves. Hundreds of sick people—blind, crippled, paralyzed—were in these alcoves. One man had been an invalid there for thirty-eight years. When Jesus saw him stretched out by the pool and knew how long he had been there, he said, "Do you want to get well?" The sick man said, "Sir, when the water is

stirred, I don't have anybody to put me in the pool. By the time I get there, somebody else is already in." Jesus said, "Get up, take your bedroll, start walking." The man was healed on the spot. He picked up his bedroll and walked off. (John 5:1–6 MSG)

This man who had been an invalid for thirty-eight years had identified himself with his condition. He obviously had people attending to him: dressing, bathing, and feeding him. However, when he was confronted with Jesus's question about *wanting* to be healed, he used blame and self-justification: "I don't have anybody to help me into the pool, so somebody else always gets there first." The question is *who* would this man be if he were well and *what* would he have to give up?

Counselors call this secondary gain. What do you lose by turning your present suffering loose? Who are you if you are not defined by your past pain and suffering?

> When we give up blame, "poor me" stories, or unrealistic schemes about how things will change in the future, we have the potential to live in the present and come face to face with the mystery of our existence. Only then can we become who we already are and live in the present.

In this case, growth is not the outcome of changing something or becoming something; it is a matter of subtraction rather than addition. It is the elimination of the outdated, overly developed, destructive defense mechanism that causes us to live like victims.

Ways People Describe Living on Purpose

Being completely in the moment can be described by the following feelings:

1. resourcefulness
2. boldness
3. energy
4. totally absorption
5. excitement
6. fulfillment
7. passionate for work
8. in tune, in the flow, in the zone
9. work seems effortless
10. life is fun

What were you doing the last time you experienced these feelings?

Keys to Unlocking Your Purpose

1. Stay open and thankful for what you already have

Gratitude is the elasticity of the soul; the more you exercise it, the greater its capacity to receive. To live in regret for what we don't have, didn't do, or wish we had done is to focus on our lack of potential and purpose. It causes us to lose sight of the abundance of our potential, and limits our imagination about what is possible. The wisdom of the psalmist was his continual focus on thanksgiving. He never allowed mistakes and regrets to be the measure of his future.

The attitude or spirit of ungratefulness—which is often manifested through bitterness, anger, grudges, and regret—releases negative energy into our physical bodies that sabotages our ability to unlock doors to our purpose and potential. Yes, what you allow yourself to think about and the emotions you allow yourself to experience influences how your mind functions and your physical body operates.

According to researchers, the physical body is directly affected by the immaterial mind. Our thoughts, attitudes, and beliefs directly influence how the physical brain controls the body's physiology. Thoughts can activate or inhibit the ability of our cells to produce protein, which results in either increased or drained energy levels.[15]

If we understand that our negative thoughts and attitudes consume energy as much as physical exertion, we will gain insight into our fatigue and lack of motivation.

An attitude is a habit of thought that is connected to an emotion. This can be a positive or a negative emotion; for example, what is your habit of thought about your workplace? Is it positive or negative? If you have a positive attitude when you think about your work, your energy level will go up; if you have a negative attitude, your energy level will go down.

When we change our attitude and vocabulary from words of regret, anger, and bitterness and develop an attitude and a vocabulary that includes words of gratefulness, we actually gain instead of burn energy: "It is a beautiful thing, God, to give thanks, to sing an anthem to you, the High God! To announce your love each daybreak" (Psalm 92:1 MSG).

"Oh, thank God—he's so good! His love never runs out" (Psalm 107:1 MSG).

2. *Trust the process*

Patience is the virtue everyone would like to have but no one wants to wait for. When we move from an attitude and lifestyle of regret, bitterness, and grudge holding, we want to see immediate results. I am often asked, "How long does it take to make life changes?" My response is, "You can't hurry growth, but you can slow it down." Then I remind the person to trust the process.

Learning the patience and wisdom of a farmer can help us through this process. The seasoned farmer knows the process of tilling the ground, fertilizing, planting, and watering his potential crop. He knows the seed he is planting, the soil and the climate, and he leaves nothing to chance. He understands there are seasons of planting and seasons of waiting before the season of reaping. He knows to watch for certain insects and other crop destroyers and defends his potential harvest.

When patience is based on knowledge, it is much more effective. When we know the seeds we plant—our vision, purpose, and destiny—and then nurture them with the right fertilizer—thoughts, books, seminars, training, etc.— we are preparing for our harvest. I tell my seminar students, "I can tell where you will be five years from now by the books you're reading and the teachers you are listening to." If we are not tilling the soil of our minds, planting seeds for growth, nurturing and watering our dreams and destiny, we will not have a harvest. "You see farmers do this all the time, waiting for their valuable crops to mature, patiently letting the rain do its slow but sure work. Be patient like that. Stay steady and strong" (James 5:7–9 MSG).

3. *Avoid the victim mentality*

When I confronted one of my students about using victim language, she retorted, "I *am* the victim!" With a few exceptions—such as rape, crimes committed against us, and prevolitional abuse (child abuse), etc.—we volunteer for most of our abuse. Regardless of the cause, in all cases of victimization there comes a point when we have to take the responsibility for our healing.

The victim mentality can become our excuse for remaining in our present circumstances. When we complain about something we are unwilling to do anything about, we are playing the victim. When we continually blame other people for chronic negative circumstances, we are playing the victim.

Victim language always has a negative qualifier: "I don't have enough education"; "I didn't go to the right school"; "I didn't get a chance for life"; "I was abused," etc. These things may all be true, but what happened to you is not the biggest problem. The larger issue is what you *allow* it to do to you.

There are many books, movies, and stories about people who overcame abuse; the one thing they all have in common is they had to make peace with the past to claim the future.

The scriptures state that when we understand God's love for us, we are empowered to overcome every challenge we encounter in life: "In all these things we win an overwhelming victory through him who has proved his love for us" (Romans 8:37 Phillips).

4. *Listen to the Holy Spirit*

We all carry on continual internal dialogues with ourselves. These intrapersonal conversations are the internalization of our parents' or caregivers' voices. It is like a tape recorder going off in our minds when something triggers old thought patterns. We make a mistake, and the tape player goes off: "You can't do anything right"; "you're an idiot"; "you will never amount to anything," and so forth. These preprogrammed internalized thoughts keep us from unlocking our purpose. These thoughts and statements must be replaced with new, positive affirmations that become a part of our new thought processes.

When we learn to listen to the voice of our Creator, we begin to understand the difference between our voices or belief systems, other peoples' voices or opinions, and the guiding voice of the Holy Spirit. However, God's voice can be drowned out if we do not understand who he is in our lives and or erroneous theology.

Which voice do you listen to—the condemning, judgmental, shaming voice of the flesh, or the encouraging, uplifting, empowering voice of the Holy Spirit? "I will always guide you. I will satisfy your needs in a land that is baked by the sun. I will make you stronger. You will be like a garden that has plenty of water. You will be like a spring whose water never runs dry" (Isaiah 58:11 NIRV).

If you get rid of unfair practices, quit blaming victims, quit gossiping about other people's sins; if you are generous with the hungry and start giving yourselves to the down and out, your lives will begin to glow in the darkness, your shadowed lives will be bathed in sunlight. *I will always show you where to go. I'll give you a full life in the emptiest of places*—firm muscles, strong bones. You'll be like a well-watered garden, a gurgling spring that never runs dry. (Isaiah 58:9–12 MSG; italics added)

5. *Move toward your goal*

Have you ever said "I will never . . .," and then find yourself doing the very thing you thought you would never do? I said I would never move to Arizona. But my wife, Sharon, and I moved to the state in 1989, and our years there have proved to be the most productive of our lives. Our points of resistance may be indicators of our purpose and calling. I am not just talking about where we live or work; your point of resistance may be the people you avoid.

One of my students found herself working with a group of people she always shunned, in a nice way, of course. Once she moved beyond her point of resistance, she found joy and relationships she never knew were possible. It's not that her life was bad before; on the contrary, her life was very good, but in her own words, "It has gone from good to great."

The Holy Spirit is the great alchemist; he takes all the things in our life, mixes them together, and brings forth something new and better.

Paul the great biblical writer, teacher, and leader knew that growth is always about going beyond our current boundaries:

> I'm not saying that I have this all together, that I have it made. But I am well on my way, reaching out for Christ, who has so wondrously reached out for me. Friends, don't get me wrong: By no means do I count myself an expert in all of this, but I've got my eye on the goal, where God is beckoning us onward—to Jesus. I'm off and running and I'm not turning back. (Philippians 3:14 MSG)

Putting Your Face into the Future

Here is an important question: what are you arguing with God about?

I first heard this phrase and saw it applied at a Lance Wallnau seminar. Since then, I have used it in some of my seminars and workshops and found it to be very effective. While conducting a Life Impact workshop in Brazil, I asked for anyone in the audience to tell me his or her passion. One young man's hand shot up so fast, I was certain he really knew what it was. I called him upfront and asked, "What is your passion?" He responded without hesitation, "Learning languages." I learned that he knew a couple of languages other than his native tongue, and English was one of them.

I asked, "Where do you see yourself three years from now?" Again, without hesitation, he said, "London, England." I asked, "What are you going to be doing there?" He said, "Teaching young people about God's love." The passion with which he spoke convinced me that he was on his way. I asked, "Have you ever been to London?" "No," he replied, "I've never been out of Brazil."

I told him to close his eyes and describe a place in London. He described what seemed to be an old church building. Since I had been to London and visited some of the old cathedrals, I had a good idea about what they looked like. His description was so clear, you would have thought that he had been there himself. He told me what it sounded like, what it smelled like, felt like, and how many young people were there. He actually experienced his desire in his imagination.

When he finished, I said, "We've got your face there; now, we just need to get your body there too." Remember, I'd asked where he wanted to be in three years. When I returned to Brazil one year later, that young man's brother came running up to me and said, "You won't believe where my brother is. He is in London doing exactly what he described last year when you were here." I was surprised that it had only taken one year for him to begin living his dream.

Here is the backstory: following my seminar, this young man, Paul, got a job with an international company. His language skills afforded him the opportunity to work in London. There, he attended a church that offered a young adult retreat. Can you guess who the main speaker was? You got it—Paul. He was living what he had dreamed. It took only one year for his body to catch up with his image of the future.

Remember Liz, the timid actress I described earlier in the book? When she recounted one of the moments from her past when she felt most alive, I asked her to "put her face into the future" and then describe her vision. She told about a powerful moment on stage and gave details that incorporated all five senses: how it felt, the silk lining of the full-length mink coat she wore, the sound of her voice over the fabulous sound system, the applause of the crowd, the smells in the room, and the taste of satisfaction that accompanied all of the above. However, at every audition since that time, she'd only received rejections. I asked, "Who shows up for those auditions? The lioness on stage from your past or the timid little girl you presented here today?" She responded, "The mousy little me. I'm afraid of the lioness that is the true me."

> "We are often more afraid of our strengths than we are of our weaknesses."[16]

Back to the Future

Going "back to the future," to borrow a title from an old movie, is one way to find our purpose and destiny. Think back to the moments that gave you the most energy, the most excitement, and the greatest sense of belonging. These are the windows that display your future. Unfortunately, we often ignore these passions as unrealistic desires or turn them into hobbies while we set out to make sensible careers that drain our energy rather than replenish it.

What do you wish you had done—studied another language, learned to play an instrument, wrote a novel, built something? The list of our secret desires goes on and on. A wish is something we think about but never actually do anything about. It is like a kid looking through a catalogue and wishing he could have what he sees.

> When passion and effort are added to our wishes, they become desires.

God said he would give us "the desires of our hearts," however; there is no such promise for the wishes of our minds. The psalmist declared, "May God answer you in time of trouble. May he send you reinforcements from heaven. May he send you fresh supplies. May he give you the desires of your heart and accomplish your plans" (Psalm 20:1–4, author's paraphrase).

Even as you are reading this promise, I believe God is sending reinforcements with provisions for your purpose: a fresh supply of energy, passion, and determination. Will you receive it? He will give you *your* heart's desire and the resources to accomplish *your* plans. Why? Because when you get in touch with *your* purpose, you are walking in his plan for your life.

Take heart; be encouraged. You are not reading this paragraph by accident. There is a divine purpose in what is happening at this moment in your life. I believe God wants to make all things work for our good, but that is dependent on our decision to love him and answer that call. Even now, he is turning things around. The only limitations to finding and fulfilling your purpose are the limits you impose upon your personal growth.

Get Your Head Out of Your Buts!

Another possible indicator of our purpose is found at our points of resistance. This is opposite to the kinds of indicators for finding your purpose previously mentioned: take note of the things you expect from others that you will not do yourself.

One of my students, who was looking for her passion and purpose, finally told me that her passion is to teach. But she said, "I want to teach, but . . ." "I could teach, but . . ." I told her that if she got the *buts* out of her head or her head out of her *buts,* she could fulfill her purpose, passion, and destiny. She stepped out bravely and is now living out her calling.

Another example involves my oldest daughter. At the time of this writing, she is finishing her master's degree in early childhood education. Since she has more than twenty years' experience in the field, she is far ahead of her peers and already has several job opportunities. Previously, when we talked about her future, she would tell me what she did not want to do. She'd talk about teaching opportunities that interested her, then close the conversation with statements like "But I don't want to teach; there is not enough money in teaching." No one had expressed either a positive or a negative opinion whether or not she should teach. This was an obvious indicator of resistance.

One day, she called her mom and said, "I know what I want to do. I want to teach; that is my passion, purpose, and destiny!" A few days later, she received an e-mail asking her to teach summer classes at a university near her home. Months before she graduated, she was already fulfilling her purpose.

Take a moment right now to remember the last thing you said you could not do. Could it be that you too have developed a point of resistance, something that you think you can't or shouldn't do, or find it crazy to even consider doing? Think about it, and if this chapter has resonated with you, perhaps you should reread it.

> Possibly all you really need to do to know your passion, purpose, and destiny is to get your head out of your buts.

Section 3

Chapter 9

Living Beyond Your Personality

Don't become a prisoner to your personality.

At this point, you have gained insight into the various personality styles and should have some understanding of your own behavioral style. You may know that we can borrow traits from other personality types for particular occasions. But trying to live them out as if they are our own is, at best, exhausting.

To be unaware of our personality styles leaves us at the mercy of negative automatic behaviors. To be aware of who we are and do nothing leaves us with exactly the same results. However, we do not have to be slaves to our preprogrammed behaviors; we can live beyond our innate styles. To do so we must be fully awake and have not only the knowledge of other options but also the power to be transformed.

As mentioned in the first chapter, our personality styles are windows into our souls. Most researchers agree that our personality styles are mixtures of nature and nurture. We will discover in this section that our innate personality types are actually the image of God within us, although they are in a fallen state.

My goal in this book is to turn your personality profiles into tools for your transformation. I am not suggesting that you, using your personality strengths or weaknesses, can solve the problems of your personality. True transformation requires the work of the Holy Spirit within. The good news is that your essential self, the nature of God in you, is always looking for ways to manifest itself. It does not matter how dysfunctional your family was or is or what events occurred in your history. Deep within you resides the call and purpose for which you came into this world.

> "The future is not waiting for you, it is waiting within you."[17]

The first step to transformation is learning to live in God's unconditional love; this subject will be discussed in full later, but, for now, it is enough to remind you that perfect love casts out all fear: "There is no fear in love; but perfect love casts out fear, because fear involves torment. But he who fears has not been made perfect in love" (1 John 4:18 NKJV).

The path to transformation and living beyond your personality requires learning to live without heeding the inner voices of condemnation, judgment, guilt, and shame.

The Four Faces of God in Humanity

God said, "Let us make human beings in our image, make them reflecting our nature" (Genesis 1:26 MSG). The prophet Ezekiel recounts his holy vision and describes the four faces of God:

1. In front, a human face,
2. On the right side, the face of a lion,
3. On the left side, the face of an ox,
4. In back, the face of an eagle.

> . . . The wings were spread out with the
> tips of one pair touching the creature on
> either side; the other pair of wings covered
> its body. Each creature went straight ahead.
> Wherever the spirit went, they went. They
> didn't turn as they went. (Ezekiel 1:10–12
> MSG)

The four primary personalities we have discussed are a
reflection of the four faces in Ezekiel's vision. The correlation
is far from coincidental; remember, God made us in his
image.

Ezekiel's vision began like this:

> When I was thirty years of age, I was living
> with the exiles on the Kebar River. On
> the fifth day of the fourth month, the sky
> opened up and I saw visions of God. (It was
> the fifth day of the month in the fifth year
> of the exile of King Jehoiachin that God's
> Word came to Ezekiel the priest, the son of
> Buzi, on the banks of the Kebar River in
> the country of Babylon. God's hand came
> upon him that day.) I looked: I saw an
> immense dust storm come from the north,
> an immense cloud with lightning flashing
> from it, a huge ball of fire glowing like
> bronze. Within the fire were what looked
> like four creatures vibrant with life. Each
> had the form of a human being, but each
> also had four faces and four wings. Their
> legs were as sturdy and straight as columns,

> but their feet were hoofed like those of a calf
> and sparkled from the fire like burnished
> bronze. On all four sides under their wings
> they had human hands. All four had both
> faces and wings, with the wings touching
> one another. They turned neither one way
> nor the other; they went straight forward.
> (Ezekiel 1:1–9 MSG)

Whether or not you are a student of the Bible, this vision is intriguing. This young man of thirty saw the multifaceted personality of God. He saw a large dust storm—man was created from the dust of the ground, according to the Creation story. He saw lightning flashing from it and a huge ball of fire glowing like bronze. When considering this symbolism, it is easy to connect the flashing lightning and huge ball of fire to human conflicts, wars, and struggles.

His next statement brings us to what I refer to as God's personalities: "Within the fire were what looked like four creatures vibrant with life . . . each also had four faces."

- In front, the face of a man is the high I (influential) personality.
- On the right side, the face of a lion corresponds to the high D (dominant) personality.
- On the left side, the face of an ox represents the high S (steady) personality.
- On the back, the face of an eagle stands for the high C (compliant) personality.

This would be interesting enough by itself, but the relevant imagery does not stop there. As you may know, the Bible tells the story of the children of Israel wandering in the wilderness for forty years after they were delivered from slavery. During that time, the Israelites were instructed to build a tabernacle of worship in the center of their more-than-two-million-person encampment. They were to assemble into four quadrants beneath huge banners. Guess what the symbols on the flags were. You got it—the face of a man (the I); the face of a lion (the D); the face of an ox (the S); and the face of an eagle (the C).

Oh, but the symbolism does not stop there. Historians who study the Israelites' tabernacle say that the large curtain or veil that separated the inner room, the Holy of Holies, bore the embroidered images of the four faces of God. In addition, the four Gospels of the New Testament reflect this theme:

1. In the Gospel according to Matthew, Jesus is represented as the lion of the tribe of Judah, a king, and the picture of the high D personality.
2. In the Gospel according to Mark, we get a picture of the high S in the imagery of Jesus as the ox or servant.
3. In the Gospel according to Luke, he is frequently referred to as the Son of Man, the high I personality.
4. Finally, in the Gospel according John, we see the image of the eagle or the detail-oriented high C.

To recap, the four faces of God are found in five places: Ezekiel's vision of humanity, the way the Israelites were instructed to set up camp in the wilderness, the veil of the tabernacle, the four Gospels, and, finally, in you and me.

> Therefore, it is important to understand that your unique personality behavioral style is not solely yours at all; it is the signature of your Creator on your life.

The master Creator only makes originals. It does not matter how many of us have similar personality styles; every one of us is an original created to reflect the image of God on this world. Yes, we have flaws and we are not perfect reflections; nonetheless, we are created in his image.

Having taught this material in more than fifteen different countries on three continents among many different ethnic groups, I have found that the personality styles are universal.

There is one more important image in Ezekiel's vision we need to consider: the wings. "The wings were spread out with the tips of one pair touching the creature on either side; the other pair of wings covered its body" (Ezekiel 1:11 MSG).

While we do not have wings, per se, we do have a need to be connected with one another. Without healthy connections or relationships, we do not have good spiritual, emotional, or physical health. Notice the second pair of wings in the verse from Ezekiel were covering or hiding the self, which is symbolic of the subconscious defense mechanisms we use to hide our *real* selves from others.

> True friendship is the pouring of one personality into another.

Chapter 10

Are You Growing Up or Down?

> The more self-awareness we have, the more
> of God's wisdom we can walk in.[18]

At this point, it is important to examine what I call ego boundaries. Most people desire spiritual, personal, professional, and relational growth. However, we don't always know what that growth is supposed to look like or how to get from one level of growth to the next.

The Ego Boundaries of High D Personality Types

Growth opportunities usually are found around our fears, points of resistance, and negative experiences. Every stimulus that reveals an old destructive pattern of behavior is an opportunity for growth or degeneration, a chance to grow up or down.

For high D personality types, the opportunity to grow up presents itself when they fear they do not have enough resources to succeed with their projects or to carry out their provider roles. I saw this frequently during the downturn in the economy. Some high D personalities found themselves in situations they had never experienced before.

On one occasion, a high D type sat in my office and wept after losing millions of dollars. He said, "I don't know how to be poor. What am I going to do?" This was better than an average response for a high D, especially since he actually came to a counselor's office for help. An average or unhealthy D would have tried to take matters into his own hands and would not have asked for help. He would have been tempted to become more shrewd and self-serving in order to get the resources he needed. Perhaps this particular high D had already exhausted every avenue and was left with no other option.

The tendency for high D types on a downward trend would be to become so angry that they would be destructive to themselves and others, controlling and demanding others to shape up or ship out. The fear of losing control due to a loss of resources makes these personalities vulnerable and leaves them feeling that they are unworthy of respect. In their downward spiral, they may go on rampages, ruining everything in their path and possibly becoming physically abusive to others and to themselves. All of these actions are an attempt to regain control.

Upward growth for these types occurs when they let go of the belief that they must always be in control. This allows them to let down their guard and heal their hearts. Healthy high Ds learn that this kind of upward growth paradoxically meets the self-protecting needs of their personalities. Now, high Ds are no longer prisoners to the negative characteristic of this personality style but are becoming transformed beyond their personality behavioral pattern.

Hence, the high D no longer needs to be in charge but can become meek (strength under control) which can make him or her appear to be an S, and yet the serenity comes from a completely different motivation.

Ego Boundaries of High I Personality Types

Growth opportunities are present when high I personalities are worried about being bored, become frustrated, or are afraid that they will not have enough money, friends, fun, or anything and everything. Fears that their actions may bring them pain and unhappiness can cause them to spiral downward. At this point, high I types will try to keep themselves excited and occupied. They may try to pump up their energy by talking, joking, or pursuing new adventures, but they may also become distracted and unfocused.

Without healthy levels of self-awareness and the skills to take control of their lives, I types can become reckless by overspending, eating, partying, etc. They may spiral downward into deep depression, producing unstable and erratic behaviors.

Growing up requires these personality types to let go of the belief that they require specific objects and experiences to feel fulfilled. They must learn to assimilate their experiences and allow their needs to be nourished internally rather than seeking satisfaction from other people. This kind of upward growth helps them focus on the world of possibilities and get excited about all the things they can do. As a result, they regain their gusto through life's diverse and prolific opportunities.

As these personality types grow up, they achieve their basic desire to be satisfied and content and have their needs fulfilled. This allows them to be appreciative, ecstatic, and deeply grateful. They no longer will be prisoners to their behavioral style. Through transformation, they will live beyond their personality types. An example of a high I living beyond his or her style is one who no longer needs to be the center of attention. Healthy high I personalities may appear as Cs fulfilling God's purpose rather than their own.

Ego Boundaries of High S Personality Types

Growth opportunities for high S personalities are present when they fear that conflicts will disrupt their fragile states of peace and tranquility. The fear of having to face reality produces anxiety and ruins their inner peace. If the high S has a healthy level of self-awareness and the skills for transformation, he or she can grow up; without these tools, he or she may grow down.

The downward spiral begins when high S types set up their lives in ways that protect them from disturbing situations. They may try to lose themselves in comforting routines and habits or become preoccupied with unimportant things in order to avoid the essentials of life. They may defend the illusion that everything is okay and stubbornly resist all efforts to confront their problems. In this state, they become depressed, ineffectual, and listless. At the extreme, the high S withdraws and becomes completely unresponsive.

When high S types let go of the belief that their participation in the world is unimportant or unwanted, they can truly connect with others. They will reinforce their self-image by creating and maintaining peace and harmony in their world. When healthy, these personality types use patient and level-headed approaches to mediate conflicts and soothe others. Letting go of destructive beliefs enables them to achieve our basic desire for inner stability and peace of mind. They can become dynamic, yet serene, and alive to the present.

When high S types experience transformation, they can live beyond the boundaries of their personality. An example of this is that they no longer feel that they must live in the shadow of others, and they can appear like Ds, and step into positions of authority.

The Ego Boundaries of High C Personality Types

A growth opportunity for high C types comes when they fear that their changing feelings will not sustain their creativity. To find relief, they use their imaginations to prolong and intensify their moods. They use fantasy to bolster their individuality and make believe that someone is coming to rescue them.

The downward trend will take them to a state of extreme self-consciousness, aloofness, and deep melancholy. They will test to see if others really are interested in them. Eventually, they will be so desperate to be the individuals of their fantasies that they will hate everything about themselves that does not measure up. This causes repressed anger, which results in depression, apathy, and constant fatigue. They may attempt to provoke rescue through self-destructive behaviors or by living completely secret lifestyles that contradict their perfectionist personae.

The way to grow up and achieve health for these types is to let go of the belief that they are more flawed than others; this frees them from self-absorption. The growth process continues when high Cs learn to explore their feelings and impressions and find ways of sharing them with others.

Their upward trend is advanced by reinforcing their self-image through expressions of individuality via creativity in art, cooking, painting, music, etc. If these personality types learn to focus on their own feelings and preferences, they can establish clear senses of personal identity. This empowers them to find themselves and their personal significance, which in turn fosters stability and a sense of belonging and of being loved for who they are.

When they reach this point, they have the opportunity for a transformation that leads to living beyond their personality. For example, the high C who no longer lives under the constraint of perfectionism can appear to be a high I, living in the joy of the Lord.

The Ego Boundaries of D/I Personality Types

The following descriptors provide a typical overview of this natural combination but may not be 100 percent accurate for every individual. The D/I combination is driven by the need for significance; the D gets significance from achievement, and the I from recognition.

The growth point for D/I combination types begins with a fear that they will be overshadowed by the accomplishments of others and their efforts will not bring them the significance they desire. Consequently, they try to distinguish themselves by overachieving and driving themselves to achieve more.

The downward trend of this process produces anxiety about the positive regard of others. This anxiety may cause them to become frantic in their attempts to please others and in cultivating what they believe will be the most attractive image possible. Their self-doubts create fears that they will not be admired or desired, which leads to an intimacy problem. To save their self-image, they deceive themselves and others, saying whatever will impress people or get them off the hook. Inside, they feel empty and depressed.

Unhealthy D/I types are so desperate for attention, they will concoct any story or scheme to hide their deterioration. They do not want anyone to know how troubled they are, and they will go to great lengths to hide their emotional illnesses and misdeeds.

D/Is can move toward health by letting go of the belief that their value depends on the positive regard of others. This frees them to discover their true identities and the desires of their hearts. When this takes place, these types become self-accepting, genuine, and benevolent. They learn to reinforce their self-image by developing themselves and their talents. They are competent, confident, persistent, and exemplary in whatever they do. As they develop more effective communication, they cultivate stronger and more intimate relationships.

As D/I personality types grow up, they reach transformation and live beyond their personality by mentoring, becoming role models, and being an inspiration to others.

The Ego Boundaries of I/S Personality Types

I/S personalities are challenged in their growth process when they fear that what they have been doing is not enough and that others do not really want them around. This personality combination needs to feel close to others and to be reassured that people like them. They cultivate friendships and win people over by pleasing, flattering, and supporting them.

These personality types want to be needed. Their lives can spiral downward when they worry that the people they love will love someone else more. They attempt to claim people by putting the needs of others before their own. Proud but needy, they do not want to let others out of their sight. They become angry when they believe that others take them for granted, yet they are unable to express their hurt. Instead, they complain about their health, draw attention to their good deeds, and remind others how much they are owed. Eventually, their repressed feelings cause physical problems.

If they continue down this path, they become so desperate for love they begin to pursue it obsessively. They feel entitled to whatever they want because they have suffered so much, and they may act out their need for affection recklessly and inappropriately. The realization that they may have been selfish or even harmed others is too much for them to handle. They fall to pieces physically and emotionally and play the victim and martyr role, so that others will step in and take care of them.

I/S personalities can start the growing-up process by letting go of the belief that they are not allowed to love or care for themselves. This growth process helps them to own their feelings and needs and frees them to love others without unrealistic expectations.

When I/S personality types focus on the feelings of others with loving concern but without expectations, they achieve their basic desire to experience unconditional love for themselves and others. They become joyous, gracious, and humble. As these personalities reach the place of transformation, they become generous with their time and energy, without any expectations. They are able to be emotionally expressive and enjoy sharing their talents with others.

The Ego Boundaries of C/S Personality Types

A growth point for C/S types occurs when they fear they will lose their independence while also believing they need more support. They invest themselves in the people and organizations that they believe will help them, but they are uneasy about it. They seek reassurance and guidance in procedures, rules, authorities, and philosophies.

Lacking self-awareness, C/S personality types may grow down instead of up. The spiral begins with the anxiety that they cannot meet the conflicting demands of their various commitments, so they try not to add more pressure without alienating their supporters. This leads to anxiousness, pessimism, and suspiciousness, which cause internal conflict that vacillates between impulsiveness, caution, and indecision. This downward movement may cause a reactive behavior that increases feelings of insecurity and leaves C/S types feeling panicky, depressed, and helpless. They can harbor paranoid fears and delusional ideas about the world. They may rant about their obsessive fears and strike out at real or imagined enemies.

C/S personality types can grow up by letting go of the belief that they must rely on someone or something outside themselves for support, and instead discover their own inner guidance. The growth process is reinforced when they develop healthy a self-image by forming alliances with others and building connections through stability, dependability, and trustworthiness.

The results of the transformation process will lead them to live beyond their personality and become well-disciplined and practical, often seeing problems before they arise. They become comfortable in the decision-making process based on their personal confidence rather than distressed by fears of what others will think or because they do not have enough information. They then become truly secure with themselves, grounded, serene, and valiant.

The Ego Boundaries of C/D Personality Types

The growth point for C/D combination types occurs when they fear that others are indifferent to what they believe. Therefore, they try to convince people how correct they are by arguing their viewpoints, often at the expense of rational thinking. They become somber and driven, remedying the problems of others by evaluating their world and pointing out what is wrong. Their need to be right and in control causes them to organize themselves and their world rigorously. They become neurotically punctual and methodical but also irritable and tense.

In their downward growth, C/D types become critical of others, constantly correcting family, friends, and coworkers for not living up to their own standards. They become perfectionistic, opinionated, and sarcastic. As the descent continues, they become closed-minded, leaving no room for compromise or negotiation of their positions. They grow toward bitterness, hatred, and distrust and become highly self-righteous. They become so desperate to defend themselves against their irrational desires and impulses that they become obsessed with the very things about themselves they want to control. They may act out their repressed desires while publicly continuing to condemn them. At this stage, they cannot stop themselves.

C/D personality types grow when they let go of the belief that they have the right and the ability to judge anything and everything objectively. Another growth point occurs when they are able to approach life without emotionally reacting to it. This healthier position enables them to reinforce their self-image by living in accordance with their consciences and with reason. In addition, it helps them to achieve their basic desire to have integrity and be virtuous.

When C/Ds experience transformation, they no longer live by the dictates of the superego or with a legalistic mentality, and their self-image becomes responsive, moderate, and objective. In this state, the C/D continues to grow up and become a highly ethical, disciplined, and purposeful individual who teaches by example and is able to put aside personal desires for the greater good.

While looking at the healthy, average, and unhealthy characteristics of each personality style, you may have found some similar to your current behavior. Do not be overly concerned if you find a few unhealthy traits in yourself from time to time; we all have them.

> The goal is to develop self-awareness so that we can consciously catch ourselves in the act, and choose to make a different response. Our aim should be to grow up instead of down.

Chapter 11

The Path to Transformation, Religion Not Required

Even if you come from a highly dysfunctional family or your life has taken you on a downward spiral, your essential self—the personality and nature of God within—is still intact and looking for ways to manifest itself.

However, we cannot solve problems of personality within ourselves. The intent of the life and death of Christ was for our transformation from death to life.

The servant grew up before God—a scrawny seedling, a scrubby plant in a parched field. There was nothing attractive about him, nothing to cause us to take a second look. He was looked down on and passed over, a man who suffered, who knew pain firsthand. One look at him and people turned away. We looked down on him, thought he was scum. But the fact is, it was *our* pains he carried—*our* disfigurements, all the things wrong with *us*. We thought he brought it on himself, that God was punishing him for his own failures. But it was our sins that did that to him, that ripped and tore and crushed him—*our sins!* He took the punishment, and that made us whole. Through his bruises we get healed. We're all like sheep who've wandered off and gotten lost. We've all done our own thing, gone our own way. And God has piled all our sins, everything we've done wrong, on him, on him. (Isaiah 53:2–6 MSG)

Transformation is made possible when we are forgiven and forgive others, which lays the groundwork for changing destructive and negative beliefs that drive our unconscious behavior. This is the process of learning to love oneself and others with the unconditional love that is the very essence of God in us. This is "the renewing of [the] mind" (Romans 12:2 NKJV) and the work of every believer. We are charged to work out *our* salvation.

Be energetic in your life of salvation, reverent and sensitive before God. That energy is God's energy, an energy deep within you, God himself willing and working at what will give him the most pleasure. (Philippians 2:13 MSG)

Let me say it again: being informed is not the same as being transformed. To be unaware of your personality style leaves you to the automatic, unconscious behavior of your personality. To be aware but do nothing yields the very same result: you will remain in bondage to your personality behavioral style.

To live beyond your personality you must be fully awake, live in the present, and have not only the knowledge of other options but also the power to be transformed.

Steps to Transformation

The path to transformation and life beyond your personality requires learning to live without heeding the inner voice of condemnation, judgment, guilt, and shame. Does that sound impossible?

> With the arrival of Jesus, the Messiah, that fateful dilemma is resolved. Those who enter into Christ's being-here-for-us no longer have to live under a continuous, low-lying black cloud. A new power is in operation. The Spirit of life in Christ, like a strong wind, has magnificently cleared the air, freeing you from a fated lifetime of brutal tyranny at the hands of sin and death. (Romans 8:1–2 MSG)

The first step is learning to live in God's unconditional love, because perfect love casts out all fear: "There is no fear in love; but perfect love casts out fear, because fear involves torment. But he who fears has not been made perfect in love" (1 John 4:18 NKJV). The world and religion call us to conformity, but the Bible calls us to transformation. "And do not be conformed to this world, but be transformed by the renewing of your mind, that you may prove what is that good and acceptable and perfect will of God" (Romans 12:2 NKJV).

Dealing with the Superego

> Superego is based on conditional love: keep
> my rules and you get to be in my club.

The superego is the inner voice that condemns us for not living up to our ideal selves. It is often the internalized voice of a parent or another authority figure.

Its original function was to make us behave in a socially acceptable and safe manner. After serving its purpose, it did not retire from the scene but instead became one of the mind's most powerful agents. This inner condemning voice now keeps us restricted by limiting our possibilities. The parts of the superego that may have been beneficial when we were children are not useful to us today. Rather, the superego identifies with our preprogrammed personality styles and causes us to act in self-defeating ways.

The Ideal Self

The ideal self is a component of the superego. It developed from the expectations of parents, extended family, teachers, and mentors in addition to those imposed by the self. The ideal self also can be influenced by trauma at various stages in our lives. As we grow up, we are taught what is socially acceptable (which is not all bad) and what kind of person we should be. Words like *should*, *should have*, and *could have* are tools of the ideal self that let us know that we did not measure up and cannot belong until we do.

The problem with the ideal self is that it becomes a false self and therefore is never attainable; the bar is always raised others or by oneself. This is too often the playground of religion.

> Most church or religious cultures are unequipped to help people face the reality of who they are and empower them to take responsibility for their messes without controlling them.[19]

The unfortunate fact is religion uses guilt, condemnation, and judgment to keep its constituents in shame about their actual performances. This keeps people dependent on the wiser, more educated leaders. This is what Jesus despised during his earthly ministry. He called the Pharisees out for their excessive rules and regulations:

> After that, Pharisees and religion scholars came to Jesus all the way from Jerusalem, criticizing, "Why do your disciples play fast and loose with the rules?" But Jesus put it right back on them. "Why do you use your rules to play fast and loose with God's commands?" (Matthew 15: 1–4 MSG)

Churches and religious organizations are not the only places that use rules to ensure conformity. This practice is also common in schools, the military, families, and society in general. I am not suggesting that we do not need boundaries. I am saying rules are not the measurement of our true selves.

Our actual performances will always fall short of our ideal selves. I lost my mother to heart disease when I was seven years old. When my father remarried a year later, I tried to be the perfect child. I did not want to lose another mother. Like all high I children, I just couldn't remember to do some things, like taking off my dirty shoes when coming into the house and picking up my toys and clothes. The harder I tried, the more I messed up, or at least that was the way it seemed to me.

The false or ideal self has a punitive corrective self that endeavors to raise his or her performance. However, since it is ego driven and based on conditional love, it can never produce the desired results.

The Punitive Self

The punitive self, as you may remember, has three basic dimensions: punishment, rejection, and disesteem. Each of these is fueled by neurotic guilt, judgment, shame, and condemnation.

The *punishment* of self is an endeavor to raise performance; however, it does not work for any length of time. When internalized, it may cause depression, anxiety, or psychosomatic disorders. Punishment may become external, such as violence toward others and physical or emotional abuse.

The second dimension of the corrective self is the *rejection* of self or others. This form of punishment is rooted in the way that parents or caregivers correct children during their developmental years. The unspoken message is *you are not loved unless you live up to our expectations*. The unintended message is *you do not deserve to be loved*. Consequently, the children grow up rejecting themselves and others.

The third part of the corrective self is *disesteem*. This is the result of constantly being compared to others, e.g., *Why can't you be like your brother or sister, the other kids at school, kids at church, etc.?* Constant comparison tells us not who we are but who we are not. Carried to extremes, it produces eating disorders, performance anxiety, and hopelessness.

I want to emphasize again that none of these self-corrective attempts improves performance. In fact, they produce what the Arbinger Institute identifies as the four boxes of self-justification (adapted from *Leadership and Self-deception*)[20]:

1. The *I am better than* box: When our hearts are at war, we exaggerate the faults of others, anything that will justify us. These individuals do not see others as people, because they must view them as "less than": less skilled, less important, less knowledgeable, etc.

2. The *I deserve* box: These people feel mistreated, victimized, entitled, deprived, and resentful. The need to be right makes it more likely that they will be wrong. Likewise, the more certain they are that they are mistreated, the more likely they will be to miss the ways that they mistreat others.

3. The *I must be seen* box: This person needs to be well thought of, likeable, helpful, etc. This produces the need to be seen as the best in sports, business, family, etc. This person needs to be served by others, rather than to serve others.

4. The *I am worse than* box: These people see themselves as broken, deficient, helpless, not as good as, etc. That viewpoint causes them to become jealous, bitter, and depressed, and to see others as advantaged, privileged, blessed, etc. Because they

fear that others are judgmental and threatening, they cannot enjoy other people or receive compliments or affirmations from others.

These forms of self-justification are never effective; they only make matters worse.

Spirit-led Correction

There is a better and more effective way to achieve correction and to discover our true identities: "For godly sorrow produces repentance leading to salvation, not to be regretted; but the sorrow of the world produces death" (2 Corinthians 7:10 NKJV). Godly sorrow and distress are the results when we miss the mark of our intended purpose. This model for self-improvement leads us instead of drives us, and there is a significant difference. Sorrow, distress, or conviction leads us to repentance and to turn things around. In this model, we do not have to live on a treadmill of regret. The previous model leads to death or separation from God and others.

Dimensions of the Spirit-led Correction

First, we take ownership of the problem or issue. When we learn that mistakes are not part of our identity, it is much easier to take ownership of them. Once we accept our wrongful actions, healthy correction is on the way. Taking ownership is different from taking on the identity of the mistake. You are not your mistake or your sin!

Second, we learn to forgive and be forgiven. If our neurotic guilt, judgment, shame, and condemnation could change behavior, we would be saints already.

Third, we learn to accept God's loving discipline. Yes, God does correct us. The Bible explains in Psalms 3:12 that he corrects those he loves. However, his corrections are not about punishment but about changing a behavior for our own good. He does not punish us for doing something incorrectly but trains us how to do it right. Human punishment is often for the gratification of the punisher, but godly correction is for the benefit of the one corrected.

> My dear child, don't shrug off God's discipline, but don't be crushed by it either. It's the child he loves that he disciplines; the child he embraces, he also corrects. God is educating you; that's why you must never drop out. He's treating you as dear children. This trouble you're in isn't punishment; it's training, the normal experience of children. Only irresponsible parents leave children to fend for themselves. Would you prefer an irresponsible God? (Hebrews 12:6 MSG)

Transition

Getting ourselves from the punitive, self-corrective model to the Spirit-led one requires us to grasp what Christ did for us on the cross. He took our shame, rejection, punishment, sin, and disesteem so that we could be free from the righteous judgment of God. Understanding and receiving the unconditional love of God requires a genuine renewing of the mind. This renewing takes place in the subconscious or unconscious mind rather than just in our conscious thoughts.

It is estimated that 90 percent of our thoughts, beliefs, and values are at a subconscious or unconscious level. This leaves only 10 percent of our thoughts in the present, and most of those are about survival. This is why you cannot make significant, lasting changes by using will power or even the power of positive thinking. Too often, positive thinking is only a mask for negative, unconscious beliefs that drive behavior.

As stated earlier, our behavior is driven by our internalized values and beliefs that reside at a subconscious or unconscious level. Therefore, only Spirit-led behavior modification is effective. When we begin to understand God's unconditional love internally, we no longer have the need to be punished, rejected, or compared to others. Like everything else in his creation, we have a purpose. When we accept Christ for who he is and what he has done, we understand that he was punished for our sins; therefore, we are empowered to change. This process leads to justification by faith, instead of self-justification because of what we do or do not do. When we realize that we are justified by faith, we start learning our true identity.

> "When we know who he is, he will tell us who we are."[21]

Time to Walk on Water

The apostle Peter was a high I/D personality—impulsive, spontaneous, and boastful. The Bible says that he was shaken like a reed in the wind; in other words, he was easily swayed by the winds of popularity. However, he was the only one of the disciples to walk on water and the person who was bold enough to acknowledge that Jesus was the Son of God.

When we know who we are in Christ and who Christ is in us, we are able to put off old mistaken beliefs and value systems and start replacing them with new beliefs and values that produce true transformation. This is the tangible result of renewing of the mind. Paul, in his letter to the Ephesians, said it another way:

> . . . You have learned Christ! My assumption is that you have paid careful attention to him, been well instructed in the truth precisely as we have it in Jesus. Since, then, we do not have the excuse of ignorance, everything—and I do mean everything— connected with the old way of life [thoughts, beliefs, and behaviors] has to go . . . And then take on an entirely new way of life—a God-fashioned life, a life renewed from the inside and working itself into your conduct as God accurately produces his character in you. (Ephesians 4:20–22 MSG)

Our perceptions change when we look at life through a different lens or belief system, and our new perceptions create new feelings:

> So if you're serious about living this new resurrection life with Christ, act like it. Pursue the things over which Christ

presides. Don't shuffle along, eyes to the
ground, absorbed with the things right
in front of you. Look up, and be alert
[be present] to what is going on around
Christ—that's where the action is. See
things from his perspective . . .

Now you're dressed in a new wardrobe
[values and beliefs]. Every item of your new
way of life is custom-made by the Creator
with his label on it. (Colossians 3:1, 9 MSG)

This is not an external disguise of outward actions but an
internal belief-and-values system. You cannot change a behavior
for an extended period of time without changing the belief-
and-values system that is driving it. Paul uses the metaphor of
changing clothes, and some have mistakenly interpreted this
in an external or religious way. However, when he speaks of
changing clothes he is referring to a transformation. As we
accept godly correction, we learn to walk out the new lifestyle.
Allowing the Holy Spirit to bring new life (i.e., values and
beliefs) into the current life is the process by which we work
out our salvation with fear (i.e., reverence) and trembling.

This fear is not a neurotic guilt but reverence for the presence
of God within us. Working out our salvation is not a work
of our will power; it is the Holy Spirit, giving us the desire
and energy to allow God's plan and purpose to work in our
lives. *The Message* says it in this way:

Be energetic in your life of salvation,
reverent and sensitive before God. That
energy is God's energy, an energy deep

within you, God himself willing and working at what will give him the most pleasure. (Philippians 2:12 MSG)

The J. B. Phillips paraphrase of the New Testament expresses it this way:

. . . for it is God who is at work within you, giving you the will and the power to achieve his purpose. (Philippians 2:12 Phillips)

Each individual's purpose on Earth is not to create his or her destiny but to discover it.

Chapter 12

Escaping the Land of Status Quo

The path to becoming who you have always
been but were never allowed to be . . .

Behavior in the Land of Status Quo is preprogrammed
and automatic. The philosophical principles of status quo
are "Don't rock the boat" and "If isn't broken, don't fix it."
This way of existence is more about survival, maintaining,
and celebrating or lamenting the past than about finding
individual identity and purpose.

Status quo is a closed system that thrives on conditional
acceptance. It is a place where you can never experience
authentic transformation, because of the mechanical
patterns passed from generation to generation. Identity
comes from association.

Life in Status Quo

The Land of Status Quo also might be called the comfort
zone. As difficult as it may be, it is far more comfortable
than the alternative. It is everyday life on autopilot. It
is going through the motions of living without really
thinking about it, like driving to a familiar place without
paying attention along the way. The problem is that the
destination or outcome is always the same. The Land of
Status Quo is a little more complex than that, but the
analogy still holds true.

This place is made up of family, friends, work, school, clubs, church, etc. It is the place where we know how things function, even when they are dysfunctional. For example, a family will learn to function with an addicted or alcoholic relative, a family member with a long-term illness or disability, or an extended absence due to work, military services, or incarceration. This becomes the new norm, and the system learns to deal with life at this level.

But should anything change, everything in this system will be thrown off balance. If a family member gets sober, addiction-free, or well or returns home, the system is thrown into chaos. It is not unusual for families to force, sometimes subconsciously, a relative back into his or her previous situation just to get their lives back into balance.

I watched this process in my own family when my son-in-law worked away from home for extended periods of time while the children were small. When he left, the children would act out to find out who was in charge. When he returned, life would be chaotic again until the boundaries were reestablished.

The pressure to keep life in balance (or in the Land of Status Quo) for everyone involved creates problems. It produces everything from passive to active aggressive behaviors.

A young female adult still living at home had engaged in a lifestyle contrary to her family values and beliefs. She was dating young men with highly questionable reputations, guys she told me later she didn't really like. After a few simple questions, I discovered that she was being forced to pursue an education she disliked for a career she did not want.

Her father was a successful businessman who wanted the best for his daughter. He tried to persuade her to get a business degree so she could become as successful as he was. A single semester at a very good university confirmed that was not for her. She came home, took a job in a coffee shop, and started living a passive-aggressive lifestyle. When asked about her passion, her answer was instantaneous: she wanted to go into cosmetology. However, her father did not feel that was a legitimate career.

I suggested that she have a heart-to-heart talk with Dad and Mom to let them know that cosmetology was her passion, and she wanted to give it a try. They agreed and paid her way through school. Her demeanor changed immediately; she has now finished school and is a very successful hairstylist in a premier shop. She loves life, and her father and mother are very proud of her.

It is not unusual to find young people who sabotage their schooling or careers because they have been forced into something that was not their calling, passion, or purpose. Others finish school, get a job, and are now living lives of quiet desperation because they did not want to upset—you know what—the status quo.

Stepping across the Borderline

The decision to leave the comforts of status quo is marked by free choice, revelation, and new information. It happens when you discover that you are more than you thought and capable of going beyond what you believed were your personal limits.

> "The human mind, once stretched by
> a new idea, never regains its original
> dimensions!"[22]

Once you decide to follow your passion and discover your purpose, you can expect opposition from the keepers of the Land of Status Quo. For example, students who are the first in their families to go to college hear statements like "Who do you think you are?" and "So you think you are smarter than the rest of us!" (These are the nicer statements that have been reported to me.) Turning back and remaining in the Land of Status Quo can be very inviting, but it is also deceitful, because once you see the necessity for leaving, it is never home again, and it will never be the same.

When the children of Israel left Egypt, their Land of Status Quo for more than four hundred years, they experienced moments when they wanted to return:

> The riffraff among the people had a craving
> and soon they had the People of Israel
> whining, "Why can't we have meat? We
> ate fish in Egypt—and got it free!—to say
> nothing of the cucumbers and melons, the
> leeks and onions and garlic. But nothing
> tastes good out here; all we get is manna,
> manna, manna." (Numbers 11:4–6 MSG)

Returning to the Land of Status Quo never feels right once you leave, even if the food is free.

The Wilderness of Change

The purpose of the wilderness is to make us aware of the habitual, destructive thoughts, attitudes, and behaviors that continually sabotage our purpose and destiny:

> And you shall remember that the Lord your God led you all the way these forty years in the wilderness, to humble you and test you, to know what was in your heart, whether you would keep His commandments or not. (Deuteronomy 8:2 NKJV)

Put another way:

> Remember every road that God led you on for those forty years in the wilderness, pushing you to your limits, testing you so that he would know what you were made of, whether you would keep his commandments or not. (Deuteronomy 8:2 MSG)

The Wilderness of Change consists of order, chaos, and the spaces in between. It is here that we discover the path to true transformation. However, it is not a straight path; it has ups and downs, crooks and turns, rough and smooth places.

This place often is filled with loneliness due to the unfamiliar people, settings, and things as well as the separation from destructive and inhibiting friendships from the Land of Status Quo. It is a place of chaos because of the disruption from previous programming. New thought processes dislodge the lies you believed about yourself, and the discomfort that occurs as past wounds are healed. There is also the uneasiness that results when debilitating belief systems are replaced, self-images are changed, and a more accurate worldview is developed.

The most liberating words in the Wilderness of Change are "I was wrong." The only way to find freedom from negative, false self-images is to see them in a new healing light from the healer of all wounds. This is where the purging of negative memories and clouded vision takes place.

When God took me through a wilderness experience the first time, I thought everything I had ever believed must be wrong. I put my face in my hands and asked God to forgive me for being blinded by my past. I had been a pastor, father, and husband for many years and could not believe that I suddenly doubted everything I'd ever understood to be true. However, let me assure you, this journey is worth every difficulty encountered along the way. Before long, it will end and creates your joyous new beginning. Get ready: transformation is on the way!

As stated in chapter 11, transformation takes place with the renewing of the mind. This requires a three-way encounter: you must have a relationship with yourself and with God. Without God in the alliance, our efforts are nothing more than our personalities trying to fix our personalities, flesh trying to transform flesh.

In his book, *Spontaneous Evolution*, Bruce Lipton explains, "Using reason to communicate with and change your subconscious has the same effect as trying to change a program on a cassette tape by talking to the tape player."[23]

Genesis's record of man's disobedience in the Garden of Eden gives us insight into our need for an encounter with God. Our biggest fear is having our secrets exposed in the presence of God and others. However, until we allow ourselves to see our negative, chronic habits, we will be unable to change them:

> So when the woman saw that the tree was good for food, that it was pleasant to the eyes, and a tree desirable to make one wise, she took of its fruit and ate. She also gave to her husband with her, and he ate. Then the eyes of both of them were opened, and they knew that they were naked; and they sewed fig leaves together and made themselves coverings. (Genesis 3:6–7 NKJV)

Rather than hide and cover ourselves, we can face our issues without fear of judgment, guilt, shame, or condemnation through God's grace, mercy, and the work of the Holy Spirit.

> Our past is not our problem; it is the shame, guilt, and judgment we carry because of it. That is the problem.

You may have suffered many heartaches, have been abused, raped, abandoned, rejected, and experienced other pains that only God knows. What happened to you may not have been your fault, but your healing is your responsibility!

As you walk through the transformation process, you will discover that your past is the soil for your future growth. I have said this before but must remind you again: When you celebrate who you are *despite* your past, you are ego-driven. But when you celebrate who you are *because of* your past, you live through your soul and are Spirit-led.

At this point, the DISC personality profile is no longer merely a method for self-discovery but a spiritual reality and tool for transformation. Using this tool, we are able to separate our preprogrammed image of God from the true face and nature of God within us. Now we can join in with this prayer of David, and ask God to reveal the things he wants to change:

> Search me O God and know my heart—
> that which is inside the real me—try me,
> test me, and know my ways—how I behave
> and get along with others. If there be any
> offensive way in me—actions and moods
> that offend or hurt other people—please
> help me to change. (Psalm 139:23–24,
> author's paraphrase)

It is here, in the wilderness experience, that we encounter our true selves; this is where we become vulnerable, naked, exposed, and even broken. It is here we find out who is behind the mask.

In the wilderness, we learn about and receive our identities, just as Jesus did during his wilderness experience. Here you learn that you do not have to prove who you are, particularly key for high D and I personality types. Nor do you have to find your identity in others, as is often the case with high C and S types. Christ was tempted in the wilderness to prove that he was the Son of God. He did not fall into Satan's trap but stayed true to his identity:

Then Jesus was led by the Spirit into the wilderness to be tempted by the devil. After fasting forty days and forty nights, he was hungry. The tempter came to him and said, "If you are the Son of God, tell these stones to become bread." Jesus answered, "It is written: 'Man shall not live on bread alone, but on every word that comes from the mouth of God.'" Then the devil took him to the holy city and had him stand on the highest point of the temple. "If you are the Son of God," he said, "throw yourself down. For it is written: 'He will command his angels concerning you, and they will lift you up in their hands,' so that you will not strike your foot against a stone." Jesus answered him, "It is also written: 'Do not put the Lord your God to the test.'" Again, the devil took him to a very high mountain and showed him all the kingdoms of the world and their splendor. "All this I will give you," he said, "if you will bow down and worship me." Jesus said to him, "Away from me, Satan! For it is written: 'Worship the Lord your God, and serve him only.'" Then the devil left him, and angels came and attended him. (Matthew 4:1–11 NIV)

The wilderness experience *reveals and confirms* who we are and is never about *proving* who we are. The further along we move through the Wilderness of Change, the closer we get to authentic transformation. I want to remind you that you are not becoming someone else but letting go of the ideal self to embrace the one you were created to be.

The voices of the past trying to call us back to the Land of Status Quo eventually will fade into the background, and we will hear the inner voice of the Holy Spirit leading us into new dimensions. In the next chapters, we will sum up this process step by step. Get ready; this transformation is not of the flesh. It is not a tadpole growing into a frog but a caterpillar becoming a butterfly. This is total transformation.

Discovery, Application, and Tending the Soul

In the opening chapter of this book, I stated that behavioral personality style (DISC) is simply a window into the soul, a way of seeing ourselves in relationship to others. Like a window, it explains how we see the world and how the world sees us. This soul window, if you will, can help us know the needs of our souls. Remember, when the needs of the soul are not met, we are impoverished.

The soul is the seat of our emotions and central point of our identities. As stated earlier, it is often difficult to describe or identify. Watchman Nee stated, "To fail to distinguish between spirit and soul is fatal to spiritual maturity."[24]

Our soul was created when the breath of life came into contact with the body God created for man:

> At the time God made Earth and Heaven,
> before any grasses or shrubs had sprouted
> from the ground—God hadn't yet sent rain
> on Earth, nor was there anyone around to

> work the ground (the whole Earth was
> watered by underground springs)—God
> formed Man out of dirt from the ground
> and blew into his nostrils the breath of
> life. The Man came alive—a living soul!
> (Genesis 2:5 MSG)

The soul is the expression of one's individuality, the central point of one's personality type, and the image of God in everyone. There is a suggestion in 3 John 1:2 that as the soul prospers so does the rest of the body and the affairs of life. The applications of this verse are manifold, but nurturing the soul is of utmost importance to everything else in our lives.

The soul comprises the intellect and emotions, which arise from the five senses. Since the soul belongs to the self and reveals its personality, it is a part of self-awareness. When the needs of the soul are not met, we act out through unhealthy behaviors that stem from our personality types. The more desolate the soul, the more destructive and pathological the behavior. Examples of this are addressed in chapter 10, "Are You Growing Up or Growing Down?"

There is a point in Tyler Perry's movie *Temptation* when the main character says, "I have the money to buy anything I want but have to beg for what I need." His soul hungered for intimacy, which cannot be bought. Unfortunately, due to his wounded soul and unhealed past, he resorted to seducing and exploiting women, yet his soul's need for genuine intimacy remained unmet.

> You can never satisfy the hunger and thirst
> of the soul merely by feeding your ego.

Chapter 13

Steps to Authentic Transformation

As we become less identified with our personality, it becomes a smaller part of the totality of who we are. The personality still exists, but there is a more active intelligence, a sensitivity, and Presence underlying it that uses the personality as a vehicle rather than being driven by it. As we identify more with our Essence, we see that we do not lose our identity—we actually find it.[25]

Start Living in the Present

I have made numerous references to the importance of living in the present. Most of us avoid the present, because we do not want to be alone with ourselves. We get distracted and preoccupied by our personality types to avoid loneliness or the emotional pain of our pasts.

Living in the present requires us to learn to develop the ability to observe ourselves, including our physical and emotional reactions, the tension in our bodies, our breathing, heart rates, and the stress in our voices. Our reactions to the things going on around us in the world give us clues to the issues that need changing. All four of the personality types find this difficult to do. The high I and D avoid dealing with personal feelings. The high C and S may get lost in their unhealed emotions. However, living in the present is important work, so don't stop.

Give it a try right now by asking yourself, "At this moment, am I relaxed or uptight? How am I breathing—deep or shallow? What is my heart rate—fast or slow?"

Learn to observe what is going on around you. What sounds do you hear? What smells are in the air? What textures do you feel? What taste is in your mouth? Look for things you have not seen, heard, felt, tasted, or smelled before. Let your five senses take in the world. Do any of the things you sense bring up old memories? If so, what feelings are emerging? Do not fight negative feelings; they belong to you and have wanted a voice for many years. You may have repressed them and failed to let them be heard for fear of guilt, condemnation, judgment, or shame. Now, it is okay for these emotions to be expressed, because in Christ provision has been made for forgiveness.

Many people tell me that they have forgiven the person who wounded them, but they cannot seem to get beyond the hurts of the past. This is often due to premature forgiveness, pushed onto us by well-meaning but uninformed people. If the wound of the soul does not have a voice, all the forgiveness in the world will not heal it.

A young woman who came to my office had a beautiful seven-year-old daughter. She informed me that seven years earlier she had been date-raped by a Christian gentleman. As she told her story, she continually referred to him as a Christian gentleman. After several of these statements, I stopped her and said, "Why are you calling him a Christian gentleman? Gentlemen don't rape women." She was shocked to discover that she was unconsciously characterizing him in that way.

She was a pastor's daughter who thought she had to protect her father's reputation and guard the church from bad publicity. When she discovered she was pregnant, the women in the church did not believe her story, because she refused to prosecute the man or have an abortion. She had buried her story for seven years and married a strong believer who accepted her and her daughter.

However, her past, unhealed emotions were erupting in her present marriage. She had prayed about the situation and forgiven her perpetrator and could not understand why she was still having issues. I explained that her soul wound needed a voice, and it had been silenced. Then, I asked how she really felt about her rapist who, by that time, had been convicted and imprisoned for other rapes.

She gave her soul wound a voice, allowing it to say what it needed to say. She no longer called him a gentleman and used more appropriate names. She shared how she really felt about the church people who had accused her of lying. She expressed the shame she felt for having negative feelings toward her family and friends. As she gave her soul wound a voice in a therapeutic manner, she became lighter and freer. A short time later, a total transformation took place. Today, her daughter has graduated from college, and this woman has a great marriage, is a vibrant worship leader, and reports that life is good.

This level of work goes well beyond the usual feelings of guilt or sadness that we experience in our everyday lives. It is about the soul showing sorrow for how deeply and completely we have been separated from our true essence. This is that haunting feeling we will never be who we were created to be and the fear of being exposed for the person we have become.

Stand Still, See Who God Is, and He Will Show You Who You Are

Standing still is a way of saying "stop" to the racing thoughts that are always trying to figure out the next move. It is a way to interrupt the "what if" game our minds play to keep us from being present.

There is a great illustration of this in the account of the children of Israel's deliverance from slavery. They had departed Egypt and were headed for the Promised Land, their place of transformation. However, they were now in a difficult position: mountains were on the left and right, the Red Sea was before them, and behind them racing to intercept was an angry Egyptian army who wanted to return them to the Land of Status Quo. They immediately began to complain and cry out to Moses, "You brought us out here to die." God told Moses what to do and say:

> . . . Don't be afraid. Stand firm [still] and watch God do his work of salvation for you today. Take a good look at the Egyptians today for you're never going to see them again. (Exodus 14:13 MSG)

In their fallen states, our personality types are always looking for the answer, the next step, or the way out, instead of the way through. The next verse of this passage says, "God will fight the battle for you. And you? You keep your mouths shut!" (Exodus 14:14 MSG) The message of this scripture to introverted high C and S personality types is, "Stand firm. Stay away from criticizing. Avoid sarcasm. Just stand firm!" To high D and I types, the message is, "Keep your mouth shut! Don't try to fix it yourself." In the midst of chaos, it is difficult to think things can ever be any different and to remember to factor God into our crises.

When my wife and I went through a major transformational experience, I was not sure what would happen next. We were on our way to California for a much-needed vacation. While I drove on I-40 through the New Mexico desert, Sharon read a book that obviously touched her deeply. She wiped tears from her eyes, trying to see the pages so she could continue to read. I said, "What are you reading?" She replied, "A book by Ann Kiemel. It is so good!" I had no idea what would happen when I suggested, "Read it out loud."

As Sharon read from that simple but powerful little book, titled *I Am Out to Change My World*, Ann's words began to change mine. She had grown up in Hawaii in a mainstream conservative denomination. However, when she moved to the Midwest, her Hawaiian lifestyle did not seem conservative to her new friends. She was confused by the legalism she encountered in her new environment. She was criticized for the clothes she wore and the things she did.

Not many people claim to hear the audible voice of God, but I am completely certain that I heard him say, "She is doing more for me than you are, and she couldn't be a member of your church." In shock, I pulled the van into a strangely convenient rest stop and asked my wife to continue reading the book. At that point, I left the Land of Status Quo and entered the Wilderness of Chaos. My church was going through a transitional season due to numerical growth resulting from the birth of the charismatic movement.

A number of mainline denominational people who had received the Holy Spirit had started attending our church. They did not look or act like our traditional crowd. The women wore makeup, jewelry and, God forbid, some even wore pants, all of which were prohibited at that time in our church world. My church board was very concerned and told me that I should be ready to deal with this when I got home from vacation. The Holy Spirit was right: Ann's habit of wearing shorts on the tennis court and pants while riding a bicycle would cause her to be shunned in our church. I realize to some this sounds humorous, to others ridiculous, but some know exactly what I am talking about.

A transformation began in my wife and me that day on the side of the road in New Mexico. I spent the next two weeks seeking God, letting God seek me, and going through my own metamorphosis. Many of my values and beliefs were internalized as a result of the way I was raised. Another voice in me insisted that I was not hearing from God or the Holy Spirit but that I was rebelling against what I had been taught. That negative voice represented the voices from the Land of Status Quo, trying to keep me in bondage to negative beliefs of the past.

It is no understatement to say that I had entered the Wilderness of Change. I thought everything I had ever believed and valued was wrong. When I tried to reinforce my old positions, I found them empty. I did not know what to do, so I stood still and waited for the Lord to direct me.

It was not long before the Holy Spirit guided my wife and me to make a major change. I resigned from the church that I had spent the past eleven years building, uprooted our two girls, and left for California with no job, no place to live, and no idea what the future held. That was in the 1980s, and our lives since then have been the most incredible journey, as I finally became acquainted with the stranger behind the mask.

Be Open, Teachable, and Adaptable

In an earlier chapter, I told you that the transformative language necessary for finding our true selves is the confession "I was wrong." This refers to some of those entrenched dogmatic beliefs that are too often like prison bars around our growth processes. Erwin Raphael McManus states in his book *Wide Awake*, "In times of crisis [chaos], it is our willingness to be adaptable that distinguishes us. Conviction is a popular excuse for rigidity, but faith should actually make us more pliable, not less."[26]

As strange as it sounds, one of the functions of the superego is to separate us from the essence of our true selves. Operating out of our subconscious, preprogrammed behaviors keep us from living in the present and limits our experience of ourselves. Consequently, when self-awareness does not fit the self-image, we reject it, no matter how positive it may be.

C. S. Lewis captures the essence of this in his classic *The Screwtape Letters*. Writing in the third person, as though he is the experienced demon, he exposes the devil's greatest fear:

> When [God] talks of them losing
> themselves, he means abandoning [their]
> self-will; once they have done that, he really
> gives them back all their personality, and
> I am afraid, sincerely, that when they are
> wholly his they will be more themselves
> than ever.[27]

The enemy of our souls will use every means possible to keep us from being the ones God created us to be. If we are going to fully discover our true selves and completely fulfill God's plan for our lives, we must remain open, teachable, and adaptable.

After resigning my church, I did not know what would come next. During this time of searching, I accepted the pastorate of a church in California and enrolled in graduate school. I earned two master's degrees in counseling—one in pastoral counseling and another in marriage, family, and child therapy.

However, there was still some of the Land of Status Quo left in me. I was an angry pastor, father, and husband. Every Sunday afternoon, I had to deal with my anger. Finally, I told my family that I would not go to lunch with them on Sundays because it was too stressful and I was too miserable to be around.

Then I received an invitation to attend a four-day Personality Plus training seminar. My wife finally persuaded me to attend, and I fulfilled all the requirements. I was not sure why I was going, but my wife thought it was a good idea. (I often say that I sometimes don't know the difference between the leading of the Holy Spirit and the suggestions of my wife.) I was about to enter another world of chaos, another wilderness journey.

I thought the training course was a bit beneath me. After all, I had completed two master degree programs and had been awarded an honorary doctor of letters. What could a four-day seminar teach me that I did not already know? During the first class, we were asked to introduce ourselves using the results of our personality profiles. I introduced myself as a pastor and said my profile revealed I was a high C (melancholy) with a secondary D (choleric) personality type.

The instructor, Florence, asked to see me after the class; she asked why I thought I was a C personality. This was when I found out what God was after. "Well," I said, "I have two graduate degrees and have taken all of the personality profiles, and they have determined that I am a high C (melancholy) personality type."

At the end of the week, she asked again what I thought my personality type was. Now my answer was "I am totally confused. I don't know who I am." She encouraged me to be open and flexible about what was happening in me and to look at my childhood pictures when I got home.

Those pictures revealed that I'd been a different person before my seventh birthday—a happy, laughing child full of life. The bright eyes and big smile revealed a high I behavioral style rather than the serious high C mask I wore after that point. When you try to be someone you are not, frustration, anger, and disappointment rule your life, as I had discovered.

When I removed the high C mask, powerful things took place. My anger level came down, and my need to be perfect subsided as my life actually changed from the inside out.

I began to mask between the ages of seven and twelve. My mother passed away from heart trouble when I was seven. When she was ill, shortly before she passed away, all of the relatives came to our tiny five-room house. They put the kids, myself included, in the only available bedroom to entertain ourselves while the adults attended to Mom and to one another, but they did not tell us about her impending death.

The stress level was obviously high. While my two cousins and I were playing in the small bedroom, we would often get too loud, and my aunt would tell us to quiet down. High I personality children want to be good, but they don't always remember to be good. So the noise level would soon rise again to unacceptable levels, and she would come in and scold us.

On the occasion of her final reprimand, she brought me to the door and said sternly, "Allen, if you don't be quiet and stop having so much fun, your mother is going to die." Her very next conversation with me was to tell me that my mother had, in fact, died. My adult mind knows that she was under stress and did not realize what she had said, but my seven-year-old mind was sure I had caused my mother's death by being too loud and having too much fun.

The pictures of me after that time reveal a completely different person. I look like a frightened high C who was trying to do everything correctly, and that became the pattern for my adult life. I could not always successfully mask my I behavior style, and that failure caused me to be angry. I am not telling you this story to stir up your sympathy and emotions. I am telling you this because this story, in some form or another, is also *your* story. Each one of us tries to become an ideal self when we do not know who we are supposed to be. I am happy to report that my mask came off, and I now like the guy who was behind the mask.

I had to get honest about myself and face the conflicts in my emotions. Prior to my healing process, having fun filled me with guilt, condemnation, and shame. So anger and frustration was all that was left for me, and those emotions I could do very well.

> Emotions do not know the difference between past and present. When an unhealed, subconscious wound is triggered, bottled-up emotions erupt into the present.

Chapter 14

More Steps to Authentic Transformation

Erwin Raphael McManus says,

> We become dogmatic as a result of fear . . .
> not faith. Faith keeps you flexible and
> postured for change. Faith ignites courage,
> not conformity. Fear seeks to control; faith
> seeks to create. Don't confuse being rigid
> and unchanging with having convictions.[28]

To have authentic transformations, we must have the flexibility to change and experiment outside our belief systems or boundaries of resistance. The kingdom of God is not a china closet filled with irreplaceable objects: it is filled with imperfect people made righteous through Jesus Christ.

You may remember that your points of resistance are the boundaries to your growth. When we say that we will never do something, we have set limits to growth in that area. Part of any educational process, formal or informal, is to question our beliefs. (Remember, at least 90 percent of our beliefs and values were established before we were six years old.) Doesn't it follow that some of those might be outdated? Hey guys, do macho beliefs stop you from experiencing your emotions and the emotions of others? If so, your world is very small and probably getting smaller.

Open Up

I challenge you to move into a condition of openness through this exercise:

1. Go to a quiet place where you will not be disturbed for at least thirty minutes.
2. Relax your body. Become aware of your breathing, heart rate, and the tension in your muscles. Try breathing deeply and relaxing. Listen to what your body is telling you. What are the thoughts going through your mind? Are you restless, agitated, or just lost in your thoughts? Take note of anything you notice while being in the present.
3. Now, quiet the chatter in your mind. This may be a bigger challenge than you think. I am not asking you to empty your mind. Rather, I want you to bring your mind into focus.

While contemplating on the following verse, place your life before God. Attach as many of the five senses to this meditation as possible: sights, sounds, taste, smells, and touch. One client baked cookies while memorizing the verse. Another cooked and tasted the food while playing a recording of the verse and made a list of things for which she was thankful. The power of this exercise is to get these words and the spirit of gratitude into the subconscious and unconscious mind so that tastes, smells, sights, sounds, and touch will trigger this positive experience instead of a negative memory or thought process from the past:

> So here's what I want you to do, God
> helping you: Take your everyday, ordinary

life—your sleeping, eating, going-to-work, and walking-around life—and place it before God as an offering. Embracing what God does for you is the best thing you can do for him. Don't become so well-adjusted to your culture that you fit into it without even thinking. Instead, fix your attention on God. You'll be changed from the inside out. Readily recognize what he wants from you, and quickly respond to it. Unlike the culture around you, always dragging you down to its level of immaturity, God brings the best out of you, develops well-formed maturity in you. (Romans 12:1 MSG)

Be Present

Here is another great exercise to bring your mind into the present:

1. Allow your heart to become more sensitive to yourself and others. Remember, there is no judgment, no condemnation, and no shame here; just compassion for yourself and others.
2. Now open up the inner qualities and resources that can help you grow. Pay attention to which voice or voices you are listening to: the condemning voice of the punitive self or the loving, corrective voice of the Spirit. Are you hearing the discouraging voices of the people from the Land of Status Quo or the voices of those who have gone before you, saying, "Come on; you can make it"?

3. Are you thinking, *I have tried before and failed*? Or do you believe that change is on the way; are excited and filled with anticipation? Do you take past failures personally and allow them to narrow your expectations, or are you falling forward by realizing that you have learned from the past? Now, you are moving forward. The greatest characteristic of high achievers is a life of expectation: they expect good things to happen.

Get a Mentor

Find someone who is where you want to be and is willing to mentor you. This person must not be judgmental, critical, or cynical. Together, create a plan for growth, and periodically review your progress.

To achieve superior performance, evaluate the following personal skills. Create an action plan to address those areas where growth is needed:[29]

- Self-awareness: the ability to understand your moods, reactions to your environment, and the effect your reactions have on others. This includes interpersonal skills, how you relate to others, and how they perceive you.
- Intrapersonal skills: how you relate to yourself, your internal self-talk, and your general attitude toward yourself.
- Personal effectiveness: how you follow through with your commitments, self-regulation, how you correct yourself, and how you receive correction from others.

- Motivation: the passion to pursue goals with energy and persistence, to work for reasons that go beyond money or status.
- Sabotaging behaviors: things that get in the way of your success.
- Social skills: the ability to manage relationships and build networks by finding common ground and building rapport.

Some people are blessed with healthy families that provide structures for personal growth and development, while others need to seek help from a qualified mentor or professional counselor.

A word of caution: do not accept the counsel of someone just because of friendship, although the right friends can be helpful. Likewise, do not select someone merely because he or she is a counselor; get references. Other helpful resources include personal therapists, life coaches, and small support groups. Remember, people cannot lead you to a place they have never been.

Finding Help

Get the right kind of help and support. The more support we have for personal growth and development, the easier the process will be. It is essential that there is a plan in place. The tools that we provide at Life Impact are based on extensive research and are approved by Target Training International (TTI) in Scottsdale, Arizona. We use three profiles as a baseline to start the growth process: the DISC Assessment, which identifies behaviors; the Values and Motivators Profile, which identifies what drives our behaviors; and the

Emotional Quotient Profile, which helps us understand our emotional development.

Personal growth must be planned; identifying sabotaging or conflicting beliefs and values is one of the most important things you can do to develop your growth. Growth is not automatic; it does not necessarily come with experience. The old adage "practice makes perfect" is only true under the right circumstances. If we keep repeating the same behaviors over and over again, we will just continue making the same mistakes.

I used to practice my golf swing at the driving range, but all I ever accomplished was a better slice. It took a coach to show me what I was doing wrong and how to do it right. That is the only kind of practice that will change the outcome. You can read all the self-help books and listen to all the motivational speakers in the world, but information alone does not produce transformation.

Be Aware

Now that you are in the process of transformation, look at everything occurring in the present as something you need to deal with right now. Remember, in the Wilderness of Change, everything has a purpose. Each and every thing that comes to your attention from your heart or mind is raw material to be used for your personal growth and transformation.

It is a common tendency to flee from what we are facing. We often escape into our imaginations by romanticizing or dramatizing the situation. We move into self-justification or even escape into spirituality or religious masking. For example, I had to release an intern because she continually used these avoidance behaviors. She was a powerful woman with great leadership potential and drive. However, when faced with her habitual sabotaging behaviors, she would escape into her "God told me" language. She would not accept correction due to her escapist behavior. Anything she did not want to face was compartmentalized into this spiritual category, which was untouchable. Unfortunately, her growth pattern spiraled downward into a neurotic spirituality.

If you have to justify or defend yourself and the things you do by saying, "God told me," you may be growing in the wrong direction.

Understand the Hunger Pains of the Soul

Learning to stay in the moment with our real-life experiences will give us all the material we need to grow. Too often, we are taught to run from, ignore, or medicate our negative emotions. These negative feelings are what I often call hunger pains of the soul. When the body needs nourishment, we experience hunger pains and have a craving for something sweet, salty, or perhaps bizarre to eat.

Every mother can remember her strange food cravings during pregnancy. Like most husbands, I made a few trips to the store during the night to bring home that exact thing my wife craved. Have you ever just stood and stared into the refrigerator, looking for something but not knowing what you wanted to eat? Perhaps like me, you ate a little of everything that was in there but still were not able to satisfy your hunger. Consider this: your body may not have been hungry. Perhaps it was your soul, and you were trying to meet the soul's needs by satisfying your body's appetite. Yes, I am suggesting the soul has hunger pains, and the things that satisfy the flesh will not satisfy the soul's needs.

The Hunger Pain to Know Our Roots

The soul is rooted in history; it reaches for a sense of belonging and to return to its roots. Movies have been made, books written, and stories told that express this theme. Anyone who was adopted, felt abandoned, or suffered a sense of loss in his or her personal history has experienced this hunger pain of the soul. Even God referred to his relationships in history when he introduced himself to Moses: "I am the God of your father—the God of Abraham, the God of Isaac, and the God of Jacob" (Exodus 3:6 NKJV).

My wife recently had a great soul-feeding experience. Officially adopted when she was four years old by a relative, she had very few visits with her siblings during her childhood and adolescent years. After the death of her adopted mother, she made contact with her family members and established a relationship for which her soul had hungered. She never knew her father but found out that he had another family; neither family knew the other existed.

A tenacious family member from the other side, with a soul hunger to find her relatives, arranged a family gathering for everyone to meet. My wife's excitement was off the charts; she was about to partake of a soul-feasting banquet that she had never thought possible.

When she arrived at the meeting place, she could feel the excitement in the air but was reluctant to leave the safety of her car. Her brother came over to her with an excitement she had never seen before. As he pointed toward the people, he said, "Look Sis, that's our family!"

Finally, she was able to get out of the car and meet everyone. The choice of the meeting place was very interesting to me. The two-family gathering was in their home state of Oklahoma at a place that contained many American Indian artifacts. The setting was perfect by conscious or subconscious choice.

Sharon had a wonderful conversation with her older brother, a high C personality type who doesn't talk much. They sat and talked for hours. He even said to her, "I just can't stop talking." This was truly a soul experience: two families coming together to share their history in a historic Native American environment, particularly since both families share a Native American ancestry. All of these ingredients made for a soul feast they will never forget.

The Hunger Pain of Sadness and Depression

Another hunger pain of the soul often manifests as sadness or depression. I realize the complexity of depression is far too broad a subject for this book. However, I want to suggest that many times our melancholy moods are actually hunger pains of the soul.

Our American culture and sometimes Christian culture treat depression as a disease. However, more often than not, Christian culture considers it a lack of faith, at best, and a sin, at worst. While depression can lead to destructive behavior, the emotion is not necessarily a result of sin or disease. David, the writer of most of the psalms in the Bible, was acquainted with depression and understood how to nurture his soul at those times:

> Why are you down in the dumps, dear soul? Why are you crying the blues? Fix my eyes on God—soon I'll be praising again. He puts a smile on my face. He's my God.

> When my soul is in the dumps, I rehearse everything I know of you. From Jordan depths to Hermon heights, including Mount Mizar. Chaos calls to chaos, to the tune of whitewater rapids. Your breaking surf, your thundering breakers crash and crush me. Then God promises to love me all day, sing songs all through the night! My life is God's prayer.

> Sometimes I ask God, my rock-solid God, "Why did you let me down? Why am I walking around in tears, harassed by enemies?" They're out for the kill, these tormentors with their obscenities, taunting day after day, "Where is this God of yours?"

> Why are you down in the dumps, dear soul? Why are you crying the blues? Fix my eyes on God—soon I'll be praising again. He puts a smile on my face. He's my God. (Psalm 42:5–11 MSG)

There are a number of references to depression in this passage. In each instance, David heard the voice of his soul and tended to its needs. This approach initiates transformation at the deepest level!

When David said, "Why are you cast down [depressed]" and "Why are you disquieted within me?" his soul was hungry for hope. So David tended his soul by feeding it hope: "*I* will hope in God" (Psalm 42:5 ASV).

When he cried out, "O my God, my soul is cast down within me," his soul was hungry for remembrance of better days. David tended his soul by feeding it: "Therefore I will remember [God] from the land of the Jordan, And from the heights of Hermon, from the Hill Mizar . . ."

"Deep calls unto deep at the noise of your waterfalls; all your waves and billows have gone over me" (Psalm 42:6–8 MSG). This speaks of David's soul's hunger for loving kindness; he needed some TLC. So, David tended his soul by decreeing, "The Lord will command his loving kindness in the daytime, and in the night his song shall be with me" (Psalm 42:8 KJV).

When Jesus preached his Sermon on the Mount, he congratulated those who allowed themselves to mourn: "Blessed are they that mourn: for they shall be comforted" (Matthew 5:4 NKJV)

Tending the soul does not mean wallowing in the wounds of the past; it means learning what the soul needs from our dark emotions. Thomas Moore states, "Some feelings and thoughts seem to emerge only in a dark mood. Suppress the mood, and you will suppress those ideas and reflections."[30]

> Considering this verse in light of our soul needs illustrates the point: I will give you the treasures of darkness and riches from secret places, so that you may know that I, Yahweh, the God of Israel call you by your name. (Isaiah 45:3 HCSB)

When we learn to recognize what our souls are hungry for, we will not need to feed them pills or anything else to drown out their voices; we will satisfy them with soul food.

The Hunger Pain of Fear

Another hunger pain of the soul is fear. I am not talking about the healthy fear of real danger. I am speaking of the pervasive fear that sabotages careers, relationships, and other areas of life. It is a state of emotional paralysis that stops the progress of living.

This hunger pain of the soul does not need to be scolded or punished; it needs proper nutrition. Scripture teaches that fear is the absence of love. When the soul lacks the proper nutrient, love, it suffers a pathological state of fear, and the cure is love.

People who live in fear have been wounded and now fear being loved and loving others. As a result, they erect a shield of hardness, anger, and toughness. However, the soul continues to suffer and manifest its pain in fear, but if we start feeding the soul what it needs, we will be made perfect in love. *Perfect* means having all the required or desirable elements, qualities, or characteristics, as good as it is possible to be. For our purposes, it might be more clearly stated as *fear needs to be loved out of us*:

> There is no fear in love; but perfect love casts out fear, because fear involves torment. But he who fears has not been made perfect in love. We love Him, because He first loved us. (1 John 4:18–19)

Chapter 15

More Ways to Tend the Soul

> Paying attention to the needs of the soul is
> living in the present.

Anxiety is a complex psychological disorder, but for this
study, we are going to examine it as another hunger pain of
the soul. When the soul has not been shown sufficient care,
anxiety becomes an issue. The soul does not respond well
to logic; it relates better to feelings. Consequently, when
the soul is not well, using logic to treat it is a losing battle.
Using logic to win a battle with a deprived soul is like using
a knife in a gunfight; you are not armed with the right
weapon to win.

Gratitude Is the Antidote to Anxiety

According to scripture, anxiety is the absence of gratitude.
Paul writing to the Philippians says to "be anxious for
nothing" and explains that when our souls manifest anxiety,
they are hungry for gratitude. When we live out of gratitude,
we live with healthy souls. These are Paul's exact words:
"Be anxious for nothing, but in everything by prayer and
supplication, with thanksgiving, let your requests be made
known to God" (Philippians 4:6 NKJV).

Learn to listen to your prayer language and thoughts. Are
you praying out of fear and anxiety or out of gratitude?
Many times people who are great at serving feel empty, void
of life, and often have illnesses for which doctors cannot

find a cause. They are so preoccupied tending to everyone else's needs that they ignore their soul's hunger pains for care and love: "Therefore humble yourselves under the mighty hand of God, that He may exalt you in due time, casting all your cares upon Him, for He cares for you" (1 Peter 5:6 NKJV).

The following passage explains this in more detail:

> Don't fret or worry. Instead of worrying, pray. Let petitions and praises shape your worries into prayers, letting God know your concerns. *Before you know it, a sense of God's wholeness, everything coming together for good, will come and settle you down.* It's wonderful what happens when Christ displaces worry at the center of your life. (Philippians 4:6–7 MSG, italics added)

People who have little to no self-awareness do not allow others to care or show love for them. This may seem spiritual, but it deprives the soul of needed nurturing. Tending the soul can be accomplished by meeting your personal needs and allowing others to do so as well.

> The ego prays out of need; the healthy soul prays out of gratitude and invites the caring work of the Holy Spirit. One sign of a healthy soul is humility.

The soul can be overly dramatic and fickle, which makes it hard to nurture. I am not suggesting that we give the soul everything it wants but rather what it needs. We must be attuned to its needs and know how to meet them, because as the soul goes, so goes the spirit and body and the affairs of life.

Ways of Tending the Soul That May Surprise You

We have identified a few ways of tending the soul through the spirit side of the triad of spirit, soul, and body. The soul is also accessible through the body, so we will look at how the five senses provide gateways for tending the soul.

Excellence is a need of the soul. Nothing touches the core of the soul like excellence. It comes to us through the arts, entertainment, and everyday experiences.

If you have ever been captivated by an excellent piece of sculpture, a painting, music, or a photograph, you were moved because it touched your soul. During the Renaissance, art became the way biblical and spiritual stories were expressed. For many, Renaissance music and art still resonates in the soul even after all these centuries.

Excellence in architecture also feeds the soul. My wife and I both enjoy the architecture of big cities, including skyscrapers and the character reflected in buildings old and new. When we lived in California, my wife made weekly trips to Los Angeles, often accompanied by other women. When they turned off the freeway into the city streets, she would frequently point at a building and say, "Look, look how beautiful that building is. Look at its windows." To her, excellence in architecture and interesting buildings are a soul feast. On one trip, a lady who had been with her several times said, "How is it you always see the beauty? Don't you see the graffiti on the walls and trash in the streets?" My wife replied, "Yes, I know it is there, but can't you see the beauty of the buildings?"

> One sign of a healthy soul is that it sees and feeds on excellence, focusing on beauty rather than trash.

Much of modern architecture serves the need to economize rather than the needs of the soul. Less-expensive designs have left many cities void of soul. At the time of this writing, Sharon and I live downtown in a high-rise building where we enjoy the architecture of newer and older buildings. We enjoy walking through the grand lobbies of hotels and bank buildings. Some of our friends will say, "What a waste of space and money. Why spend all that money on marble floors and expensive art? What a waste!" When I reply, "It's soul food," they look at me like I am crazy. Try walking through an art museum and letting the works of world-class artists speak to your soul. History and art combined is a powerful soul delicacy.

I recently had a client who was struggling to find his purpose and passion for life. I suggested that his problem might be a soul issue, not a motivation issue. He had received prayer, spent days fasting and praying, and had sought counsel from various people but still felt lost and lethargic. I recommended he find a museum and spend no less than three hours letting the artifacts of history speak to him. I didn't suggest a particular place but trusted that his intuition or spirit would lead him to the right place. He reported back an amazing experience. As a newcomer to our city, he had no idea where to go. He asked friends, coworkers, and even strangers if they knew about an interesting museum that he could visit.

Several people suggested he visit a musical instruments museum that had been open for only a couple of years. He found the place and, as I had instructed, he walked, sat, listened to music, and gazed at the instruments for hours. He told me later, "I didn't think I would be able to stay three hours, but it went by in a flash." This is indicative of a soul feast.

He went on to say that it had been one of the most amazing experiences of his life. He had not felt so alive in years. Then, he spoke about a time many years ago when he'd played an instrument. However, after a bitter disappointment that created a soul wound, he put his music down. The wound left an appetite in his soul that he tried to satisfy with something that became a destructive behavior. The powerful museum experience awakened his soul, tended to his wounds, and reenergized his life.

David Feasted on the Excellence of the Creator

> Lord, our Lord, how majestic is your name
> in all the earth! You have set your glory in
> the heavens. (Psalms 8:1 NIV)

Excellence is a word that describes the worship ministry at our church, Church for the Nations, led by B. J. Putnam and the Create Worship ministry. Pastor B. J. and his team strive for excellence in the sound and visual presentation of worship in every service. Although I am not a musician or a singer, I know when excellence resonates in my soul and brings me into the presence of my Creator. It is an awesome experience!

In contrast, some complain about the worship with statements like "It's too flashy, too much like the world" or "They are just showing off." I believe their disapproval comes from frustrated, ego-driven personalities whose souls are deprived. Their hunger pain manifests as unjustified criticism from soul wounds begging to be healed. There is a big difference between man showing off during worship and God showing up.

> Tending to the soul wound of an individual, a city, or a nation can change the environment.

The former mayor of New York, Rudy Giuliani, tended to the soul wounds of his city by restoring broken windows, painting abandoned buildings, and cleaning up the graffiti. As a result, he lowered the crime rate of the city.

We tend our souls by enjoying the beauty and diversity of nature. Sometimes I tell clients to visit a garden or a lake or go on a hike, any activity that will get them back to nature and allow their souls to drink in nature's beauty, as a butterfly drinks nectar from a flower.

People come from all over the world to gaze into the Grand Canyon; others scale mountains through great effort, or sit beside lakes, streams, or rivers to appreciate nature. Whether you live in the desert, as we do, the lush coastline of California, the tree-laden mountains of Colorado, the Smoky Mountains of the East, or elsewhere in the world, you can enjoy the unique beauty of God's creation and feed your soul. I am not talking about worshiping nature; I am speaking about enjoying what God created. Appreciating beauty in nature can lead to the value and worship of the One who made it.

You don't have to be an extreme environmentalist to recognize that the loss of our forests and other natural things is a loss of the Earth's soul. Without the beauty, diversity of color, and variety that nature brings, the Earth has no soul. According to scripture, even the Earth's soul cries out for a better day: the created world itself can hardly wait for what's coming next.

> Everything in creation is being more or less held back [from becoming all it was made to be]. God reins it in until both creation and all the creatures are ready and can be released at the same moment into glorious times ahead. Meanwhile, the joyful anticipation deepens. (Romans 8:18–21 MSG)

> But we are looking forward to a new heaven and a new earth. Godliness will make its home there. All of this is in keeping with God's promise. (2 Peter 3:13 NIRV)

We live in a world of expectation and variety

Signs of a Healthy Soul

I want to pause for a moment and remind you that we are talking about transformation at the deepest level. Our self-sabotaging behaviors are reinforced by negative or outdated values and beliefs rooted in the depths of the soul. In those deep places, our God-given personality styles often are locked away with false beliefs and create points of resistance that establish boundaries around our growth process.

I have shared a number of transformational points on my journey through the Wilderness of Change, and I would like to share another. For forty years, I was a senior pastor at a mainline Pentecostal denomination. I started at a young age and was very loyal to my organization. I thought that people who were not part of an organized church movement were rebellious, unacceptable, and out of step with God's perfect will.

While part of this organization, I had many opportunities to serve. In addition to being a local pastor, I oversaw the starting of new churches and the training of ministers. I also served as president of one of the denomination's colleges and had the opportunity to travel around the world in ministry. I mention this to let you know that serving this organization was a great experience. I have no negative feeling or complaints about my time of ministry with it.

However, one day something changed inside me. In spite of having a great church, a great staff, and an easy life in general, I became totally unsatisfied. I thought of myself as a fish in a small aquarium that constantly bumped into the glass, but I never mentioned this analogy to anyone.

One day a friend and church member came to me and said, "I had the funniest dream about you last night. I dreamed you were a fish in an aquarium, someone took a sledge hammer to it and smashed the glass, and you spilled out into the deep blue sea." *Wow!* I thought. *What is going on?*

After discussing it with my wife and daughters, I decided to resign and see what God wanted me to do. We retired, and I walked away, thinking we had a secure future with our real-estate investments. My youngest daughter, Pam, and her husband had visited the church we now attend and suggested that we try it out. I knew that it was an interdenominational church, which is a code word for an independent church, and I always said I could never attend "that kind" of church. This is a prime example of how a point of resistance can become an obstacle to growth.

We did visit, and we were so blessed by the ministry of the church that we continued to attend. After three months, we introduced ourselves to the pastor, and he asked us to make an appointment with him and the staff. I assured him that I was not running from anything in my past or looking for a job. I was just trying to find out what God wanted for this season of my life.

The rest is history; I now serve on staff, and I'm having the time of my life. *I was wrong!* Remember, "I'm wrong" are the words that get you through the Wilderness of Change.

> Tending the soul is like caring for a garden: pruning, weeding, cultivating, watering, fertilizing, and protecting the soul from the insects of our toxic thoughts and words. We must also guard against the negative intrusion of overly critical people as well as tend to the soul wounds of the past.

Chapter 16

Taking the Final Steps

> Examine me, God, from head to foot,
> order your battery of tests. Make sure I'm
> fit inside and out. (Psalm 26:2 MSG)

I have talked a lot about "tending the soul," but now it is time to take the final steps on our journey to transformation.

The Next Tool for Transformation: Cultivating a Real Love of Self

Most of this book has been about coming to know yourself, but authentic transformation requires cultivating a genuine love for yourself. We are instructed to "love your neighbor as you do yourself" (Matthew 19:18).

As a quick reminder, let's look again at the following passage of scripture:

> May God himself, the God who makes everything holy and whole, make you holy and whole, put you together—spirit, soul, and body—and keep you fit for the coming of our Master, Jesus Christ. The One who called you is completely dependable. If he said it, he'll do it! (1 Thessalonians 5:22–24 MSG)

Each individual is made up of spirit, soul, and body. When we follow the influences of our bodies, we are being led by the appetites of the flesh, and there is ample evidence that this can be a destructive path. On the other hand, if we merely follow our spirits, we will be out of balance and end up in a state of spiritual confusion. Finally, if our souls are left in charge, we will be stuck in the past and will be unable to live in the present or future.

I realize that loving your body is rarely taught in the Christian community. The church world mostly ignores the flesh and focuses on spiritual things, since it does not consider the physical body to be spiritual.

During the time of Christ, there was a prevailing belief that the body was irrelevant; it didn't matter what you did with your body, because it would return to dust. So people adopted a hedonistic, voluptuous approach to life, as expressed in the phrase "if it feels good, do it." This self-indulgent, pleasure-seeking lifestyle also is very much alive today. However, seeking physical pleasure is not the same as authentically loving yourself and it does not produce the transformation to the original self, the image of God within us, for which our soul longs. Cultivating a real love of self does not come from overindulgence in fleshly desires or, for that matter, from excessive self-denial or loathing of the flesh.

My grandson took an art psychology class, and the instructor tried to teach the students to love their bodies. She told the students to gaze at their hands and say, "This is my hand, and I love my hand." He found this a little strange and mentioned it to me. I reassured him that it was a good and valid thing to do because God made our human bodies, and they are truly amazing and deserve our appreciation and, yes, even our love.

David declared:

> Oh yes, you shaped me first inside, then
> out; you formed me in my mother's womb. I
> thank you, High God—you're breathtaking!
> Body and soul, I am marvelously made! . . .
> You know me inside and out, you know
> every bone in my body; You know exactly
> how I was made, bit by bit, how I was
> sculptured from nothing into something.
> Like an open book, you watched me grow
> from conception to birth; all the stages of
> my life were spread out before you, the days
> of my life all prepared before I'd even lived
> one day. (Psalm 139: 13–16 MSG)

You can't read David's description and not see his appreciation
for the body God gave to humanity.

God never intended us to worship the flesh by placing its
desires first, but he never planned for us to hate it either.
Some early church fathers so hated the flesh that they
mutilated themselves to eliminate their innate, God-given
drives, and some current cults do the same. The modern-
day church practices other rituals to guard against satisfying
the needs of the flesh by placing the responsibility for their
inappropriate thoughts and behaviors on someone else, often
women.

The church world I grew up in was especially hard on women:
no makeup or wearing pants, even though that was probably
more modest. Women were not allowed to cut their hair or
wear open-toed shoes; even jewelry was not allowed for fear

it would draw the attention of men. In essence, the church made women responsible for men's lustful desires, the same mistake other religions are making today.

While in much of today's church culture this sounds ridiculous, there are still groups that impose such rules on women. This was not and is not the intent of Christ's teachings. Jesus did more to liberate women than any other spiritual leader before or after him.

The greatest compliment God ever paid to human flesh was to send his Son to Earth in the form of flesh: "The Word became flesh and blood, and moved into the neighborhood" (John 1:14 MSG). Another scripture refers to our bodies as temples of the Holy Spirit and tells us not to defile these temples:

> You realize, don't you, that you are the temple of God, and God himself is present in you? No one will get by with vandalizing God's temple, you can be sure of that. God's temple is sacred and you, remember, are the temple. (1 Corinthians 3:16 MSG)

Jesus lived in the flesh without sin and took the punishment for our sins, so that in the sight of God, we could be forgiven. Volumes have been written on this subject, but my point is, hating the flesh does not produce transformation or bring you to a state of convergence. It is refreshing that some leaders of the Christian community are emphasizing the importance of getting into better physical shape. If you can't love your body for yourself, love it for the One who created you, and honor the purpose he has in mind for it.

How does loving my body help me reach my goal of authentic transformation? Failing to take care of the body is a form of self-rejection. Taking proper care of the body is a form of giving value to self. This is similar to demonstrating love to your mind and soul by removing negative thoughts and healing your emotional wounds, so that nothing can sabotage the transformational process.

You Must Be Present to Love Body and Soul

We learn to love ourselves by being present with ourselves. Loneliness is the result of not wanting to be with ourselves and spending most of our time regretting the past or fearing the future.

We get caught up in worry, fear, tension, and anxiety, which disconnect us from our bodies and emotions, and we abandon our soul, the true self. This is especially prevalent with high D and high I personality types.

When we are disconnected from our bodies, we are not in tune with what our bodies are asking for, such as enough rest, proper nutrition, and other healthy activities. As stated above, neglecting our bodies is a form of self-rejection at best and self-hatred at worst. In either case, we are neglecting the temple of God's Spirit as well as our own spirits, souls, and bodies.

> There is a direct link between the health of the soul and that of the body. The body is a reflection of the soul.

Another positive way of creating a real love for self is by cultivating personal growth and development, which is the purpose of this book. Loving yourself is living in the moment enough to face the discomforts and pains in your life. So stop and listen to what your pains of depression, anxiety, fear, or other negative emotions are telling you about yourself.

To Be Present, Observe Your Reactions

Another way of operating in the present is to pay attention to your reactions. Overreacting in ways that do not fit the current situation comes from our false selves or wounded places in our souls. Whatever stimulus—sound, touch, smell, taste, or sight—triggers the overreaction, it is tied in some way to an unhealed wound from the past that explodes into the present.

While *reactions* are preprogrammed by past pains, *responses* are actions free from the pain of the past. Until our preprogrammed reactions are dealt with and healed, no verbal commitment or positive affirmations will be able to produce change. We can say one thing with our conscious mind but in our heart believe something totally different.

What we believe in our hearts at a subconscious level is what we actually accept as true and act upon. Any statement or experience that challenges our internalized belief systems is perceived as a threat and is paralyzing to us. Having said that, it is imperative that we work on both the conscious and the subconscious at the same time. As stated earlier, if we change our stories from our past failures, disappointments, and hurts to hope for the future, if we can talk about what we do have instead of what we don't have, we can begin to change our internalized beliefs.

We are not chained to past experiences or our current way of being. We do not have to be prisoners to our personality behavioral styles. We can choose to be free from toxic experiences and step into the future.

More Tools for Transformation: Developing Spiritual Practices

Throughout the book, I have talked about our automatic, preprogrammed reactions to life, and emphasized that without self-awareness we have a limited ability to control our behaviors. We usually go through life on autopilot, which, more often than not, sabotages our best intentions. We also lose our identities as the world around us squeezes us into its mold and our internalized negative beliefs become the driving force of the lies we believe.

In his book, *The Biology of Belief,* Bruce Lipton states, "It is my sincerest hope that you will recognize that many of the beliefs propelling your life are false and self-limiting and you will be inspired to change those beliefs."[31] We can and do become prisoners to the internalized lies. When we become aware of this through spiritual practices or become conscious to our habitual, ingrained behaviors through any means, we can wake up from the trance and no longer live as prisoners to our subconscious, preprogrammed reactions.

We can become so numb to our emotional states that we lose touch with what I have called the hunger pains of the soul: fear, anxiety, depression, and other emotional stressors. We become like lepers who have lost the ability to sense pain and are unable to identify infections and other dangers that cost them their limbs and eventually their lives.

Paul Brand, an expert on treating leprosy, describes this condition in one of his patients in the book *Fearfully and Wonderfully Made*, written with Phillip Yancey:

> When Sadan first came to Vellore [the location in India where Brand practiced for many years], his feet had shrunk to half their normal length and his fingers were shortened and paralyzed. It took us nearly two years of unflagging effort to stop the pattern of destruction in his feet. Meanwhile we began reconstructing his hands, a finger at a time, attaching the most useful digits and retraining his mind to control the new sets of connections.
>
> At last [after four years of rehabilitation], Sadan decided he should return home to his family in Madras for a trial weekend. On a Saturday night, after an exuberant reunion dinner with his family, Sadan went to his old room where he had not slept for four years. The next morning when he awoke and examined himself, as he had been trained to do, he recoiled in horror. Part of the back of his left index finger was mangled. He knew the culprit because he had seen such injuries on other patients.

> During the night a rat had visited him and gnawed his finger.
>
> After several other incidents of such nature, he returned to the hospital where he and Dr. Brand wept over the incidents.
>
> Because Sadan couldn't feel any pain, he didn't wake up when the rat was chewing on his finger. He reported to Brand, "I feel as if I've lost all my freedom. *How can I be free without pain?*"[32]

I suggest that we need to feel the hunger pains of our souls to experience transformation and growth. When we are numb to those pains, like the body of a leper, we dry up and die.

This story is a little graphic; however, I and other counselors have witnessed the catatonic state of overly medicated clients. I am not suggesting that medicines do not have a place. I am saying that medication often is prescribed as a quick fix when what we should do is find out what our souls really need.

> As Brand says, "Pain is our friend." Listen to what your soul is trying to say to you. We must awaken from our lethargic state of unconscious, automatic behaviors if we want to breakthrough to convergence.

Spiritual Disciplines Awaken Us

The purpose of spiritual disciplines is to rouse us from our automatic behaviors and get us in touch with our true

God-given nature. The more we know who he is, the more we can discover who he created us to be: "Who believed [God] was who he claimed and would do what he said, he made to be their true selves, their child-of-God selves" (John 1:12 MSG).

To break out of the hypnotic state in which we automatically react to life, we need to develop a conscious awareness of and a relationship with our Creator. Most people are familiar with prayer of one kind or another. For many, it is an arduous experience wrapped in the garments of religious practice with little noticeable return on the time invested. For others, however, it has become a valuable experience, a two-way conversation with God. It can be the same for you.

The phrase "God told me" often is attached to some kind of radical action and is used to justify psychotic behavior. On the other hand, we sometimes discount genuine communication from God because we fear being called crazy. This is due to a lack of understanding of the way God communicates with us. In his book *Hearing God*, Dallas Willard quotes comedian Lily Tomlin:

> "Why is it, that when we speak to God we
> are said to be praying, but if God speaks to
> us we are said to be schizophrenic?"[33]

We live in a world where we are suspicious of those who report that they hear from God. However, developing a prayer life is like developing a relationship with someone by learning to both talk *and listen*. Scripture directs us to "pray without ceasing." *The Message* translation says it like this:

"Be cheerful no matter what; pray all the time; thank God no matter what happens. This is the way God wants you who belong to Christ Jesus to live" (1 Thessalonians 5:17).

A conscious awareness of God's presence keeps us in tune with what is happening within us and around us. In addition, when we do not know how or what to pray, God's Word promises that his Spirit will pray through us:

> . . . If we don't know how or what to pray, it doesn't matter. He does our praying in us and for us, making prayer out of our wordless sighs, our aching groans. He knows us far better than we know ourselves, knows our pregnant condition, and keeps us present before God. That's why we can be so sure that every detail in our lives of love for God is worked out into something good. (Romans 8:26–28 MSG)

Spiritual Discipline: Meditate to Elevate

Meditation is another spiritual discipline that brings us into the present. However, the meditation I refer to is *not* the kind that empties the mind of everything or takes you to an altered state of nothingness. Christian meditation focuses on scriptural promises and follows with prayers of personalized declarations concerning one's purpose and destiny.

David, the psalmist, gave us a great example of what to separate ourselves from and how to fill our minds in Christian meditation:

> Blessed is the man who walks not in the counsel of the ungodly, nor stands in the path of sinners, nor sits in the seat of the scornful [thought processes and sometimes people from whom we need to separate]; But his delight is the law [Word] of the Lord, and in His law [Word] he meditates day and night. (Psalm 1:1–2 NKJV)

The Message translation says, "You chew on Scripture day and night" (Psalm 1:2).

Pay special attention to the imagery expressed in the verse that follows the last passage: "He shall be like a tree planted by the rivers of water, that brings forth its fruit in its season, whose leaf also shall not wither; and whatever he does shall prosper" (Psalm 1:3 NKJV).

Emptying our minds is not a good idea, because it can open us to destructive patterns of thought:

> When a defiling evil spirit is expelled from someone, it drifts through the desert looking for an oasis, some unsuspecting soul it can bedevil. When it doesn't find anyone, it says, "I'll go back to my old haunt." On return if finds the person spotless clean, but vacant. It then runs out and rounds up seven other spirits more evil than itself and they all move in, whooping it up . . . (Matthew 12:43–45 MSG)

This demonstrates the benefit of faith-based counseling. Any counselor can lead his or her client to a catharsis, the emptying of negative emotions, without knowing what to put in the empty place. We can be encouraged by these words: "The peace of God, which transcends all understanding, will guard your hearts and your minds in Christ Jesus" (Philippians 4:7 NIV). Then, we are told how to fill our minds:

> Summing it all up, friends, I'd say you'll do best by filling your minds and meditating on things true, noble, reputable, authentic, compelling, gracious—the best, not the worst; the beautiful, not the ugly; things to praise, not things to curse. Put into practice what you learned from me, what you heard and saw and realized. Do that, and God, who makes everything work together, will work you into his most excellent harmonies. (Philippians 48: 8–9 MSG)

When one's spirit is in unison with the Holy Spirit, the soul is nourished and is able to feed the body with what it needs. Remember, John's prayer for his friends: "I wish above all things that you may *prosper and be in health, even as your soul prospers*" (3 John 2:1, author's paraphrase). What takes place in the soul is reflected in the body.

Spiritual Discipline: Develop Your Intuition

> In his book *The Spiritual Man*, Watchman Nee says, "Intuition is the sensing organ of the human spirit. It is so diametrically

different from physical senses and soul
senses that it is called intuition."[34]

Intuition is a direct sensing of something, independent of
any outside influence. It is knowledge that comes to us
without any help from the mind, emotions, or will. We
know through our intuition; our minds merely help us
understand. The revelation of God and all the movements of
the Holy Spirit are known to the believer through intuition.
Women tend to be more sensitive to the intuitive voice than
men are, and the Western mentality is less in tune with
intuition than other cultures.

Transformation is dependent on learning to hear the inner
voice, our spirit's voice, and our intuition, which come
through our relationship with the Holy Spirit. The prophet
Elijah had to learn to discern the voice of the Lord:

> Go, stand on the mountain at attention
> *[be present]* before God. God will pass
> by. A hurricane wind ripped through the
> mountains and shattered the rocks before
> God, but God wasn't to be found in the
> wind; after the wind an earthquake, but
> God wasn't in the earthquake; and after the
> earthquake fire, but God wasn't in the fire;
> and after the fire a gentle and quiet whisper.
> (1 Kings 19:11–12 MSG; emphasis added)

God was in the whisper, and it was in that still, small voice
that Elijah heard him speak.

Spiritual Discipline: Practice Gratitude

Here it is again; gratitude is an essential spiritual practice. We talked about it before, but now is the time to begin practicing it to ensure your breakthrough. Gratitude in the spiritual sense means learning to be thankful in everything and learning from everything. Without gratitude, we dry up and become brittle, controlled by regrets and fears.

The practice of thankfulness removes the spirit of cynicism and pessimism. It stimulates our humility and makes us magnanimous toward others and ourselves.

> Thankful people live healthier and happier lives; they are more engaging, open, and transparent.

The practice of gratitude is not an escape from reality. Rather, it stems from the belief and experience that all things really do work together for the good of those called according to his purpose (see Romans 8:28). A spirit of gratitude removes us from the trap of living like victims and empowers us to be victorious. A lifestyle of thankfulness helps us to live in the moment, to be present in the here and now.

I challenge you to stop reading for a moment and give thanks for everything around you. Pay attention to your five senses. Be thankful for everything you see, touch, smell, taste, and hear. Even if you are in a distasteful situation or a less-than-perfect environment, there are things for which you can be grateful. At the very least, be thankful for the ability to use any or all of your five senses. (Pause now to practice gratitude.)

> The pathway to transformation is paved
> with gratitude.

Nehemiah, the rebuilder of Jerusalem, assigned two large choirs to give thanks to the Lord once the city's walls were completed (Nehemiah 12:31). The Psalms are full of thanksgiving: "I will give thanks to you, Lord, with all my heart; I will tell of all your wonderful deeds" (Psalm 7:17 NIV); and "Enter his gates with thanksgiving and his courts with praise; give thanks to him and praise his name" (Psalm 100:4 NIV). Thanksgiving is the theme of the scriptures, and it certainly can be the story of our lives as well.

Spiritual Discipline: Not My Will but His Will Be Done

One of the major obstacles to regular spiritual practices is the expectation of attaining a specific result.

In *Hearing God*, Dallas Willard writes, "I fear that many people seek to hear God solely as a device for securing their own safety, comfort, and righteousness. For those who busy themselves to know the will of God, however, it is still true that 'those who want to save their life will lose it (Matthew 16:25).'" He quotes Frederick B. Meyer: "So long as there is some thought of personal advantage, some idea of acquiring the praise and commendation of men, some aim of self-aggrandizement, it will be simply impossible to find out God's purpose concerning us."[35]

When Jesus prayed in the garden before his crucifixion, he surrendered his will to the will of his Father. If you have pursued the will of God, you no doubt have discovered that the path to his purpose often takes a different turn from what you might have ever imagined.

We must guard against making this spiritual practice nothing more than another manifestation of our old selves wrapped in different garments, which is merely a transformation of the flesh by the flesh. We may change our vocabularies and switch activities but still use the same destructive behaviors. This is too often the case in many people's lives: rituals simply becomes a substitute for authentic transformation.

Experiencing Transformation

Transformation, like the other stages of our journey, is not a destination as much as a state of being. It is a departure from the Land of Status Quo, a step over the line of decision, and a move through the Wilderness of Change and into the state of transformation.

In the Wilderness of Change, we are able to separate identity by association and our desires from our wishes. In his CD series *In a Heartbeat*, Lance Wallnau says that you must guard your mental state or be dominated by someone else's. To resonate with your purpose, you have to see your face in the future and, moment by moment, adjust your walk to make it manifest that future. He goes on to say, "The funny thing about desire is, if you learn to honor desire, the heavens and God have already charted a course for you."[36]

> "Convergence occurs when passion, skill, and talent intersect with opportunity."[37]

Allen McCray

Convergence is when we are the most productive, have the greatest impact, and are energized at the highest levels. It is not a static state but a dynamic one in which we are constantly moving from one level to another. We see it when athletes are "in the zone." It occurs when you feel the power of your purpose come together with everything that is within you. It happens when actors and musicians give performances that set them apart from everyone else. It's not just what we experience but what others experience through us. You do not have to announce when you are in convergence; others will recognize it.

For me, convergence is teaching this material. It has transformed my life and my family, changed my view of the world, deepened my relationship with God, and helped me find my zone. In writing this book, many of the things I have learned, experienced, and observed in others have come together and intersected during this season of my life. When I see lives transformed in front of me and hear the success stories later, I bask in convergence.

My prayer is that through this book, I can help you find your convergence too.

> True transformation is when you can look
> in the mirror and like the person you see.